I'm so excited for this book to take you on so many adventures in and out of the kitchen. Have fun with your healthy lifestyle and kitchen experiments. Try not to take any of it too seriously. The only messing up is giving up. So if you think a recipe could use more salt or sauce, try it, track it and see how it works for you. You got this!

Love, Ilana

LOVE THE FOOD THAT LOVES YOU BACK

LOVE THE FOOD THAT LOVES YOU BACK

Weight Management Made Easy by Choosing the Right Food

100 Recipes That Serve Up Big Portions and Super Nutritious Food

ILANA MUHLSTEIN, MS, RDN

PUBLISHING GROUP

CORAL GABLES

Copyright © 2024 by Ilana Muhlstein MS, RDN.
Published by Mango Publishing, a division of Mango Publishing Group, Inc.

Cover Design: Elina Diaz
Cover Photo: Gabriel Mendoza Weiss
Interior photos: Corinne Quesnel
Layout & Design: Elina Diaz

For permission requests, please contact the publisher at:
Mango Publishing Group
2850 S Douglas Road, 2nd Floor
Coral Gables, FL 33134 USA
info@mango.bz

For special orders, quantity sales, course adoptions and corporate sales, please email the publisher at sales@mango.bz. For trade and wholesale sales, please contact Ingram Publisher Services at customer.service@ingramcontent.com or +1.800.509.4887.

Love the Food that Loves You Back: 100 Recipes That Serve Up Big Portions and Super Nutritious Food

Library of Congress Cataloging-in-Publication number: 2023941621
ISBN: (print) (hc) 978-1-68481-377-3 (pb) 978-1-68481-378-0 (e) 978-1-68481-379-7
BISAC category code: CKB050000, COOKING / Health & Healing / Low Cholesterol

Printed in the United States of America

This book is dedicated to my husband, Noah Muhlstein,
who is not only responsible for helping me complete this book and stay
on top of deadlines but is also my best friend and support system.

TABLE OF CONTENTS

Introduction   13

Breakfast   **17**

    Chocolate Cream Rolls   19

    Protein Oats   20

    Tempeh BLT   21

    Supersized Scrambled Eggs and Toast 22

    Veggie Omelet Loaf   23

    French Toast   25

    Chocolate Chip Breakfast Cake   26

    Seasonal Breakfast Boats: Papaya & Sweet Potato   29

Craveable Veggies   **30**

  Pasta Swaps   **31**

    Thai Peanut Hearts of Palm Spaghetti   33

    Three Ways to Cook Spaghetti Squash Whole   34

    Spaghetti Squash Cacio E Pepi   37

    Eggplant Sesame Noodles   38

    Pesto Shirataki Noodles   41

    Feta Pasta with Kelp Noodles   42

  Roasted Wonders   **44**

    Eggplant Parm Fries   45

    Broccoli Crunch with Ranch Dip   47

    Air Fried Mini Bell Peppers   49

    Mushroom Cap Pizzas   51

    Kohlrabi Nachos   52

    Parm Crusted Palm   55

    Basket of Fries   56

    Cauliflower Toasts   59

    Maple Bacon Brussels Sprouts   60

    Everything Eggplant "Tacos" and Mini Tortillas   63

    Tahini Teriyaki Roasted Carrots   64

Leveled Up Shishito Peppers   67

Ilana Meals Blistered Veggies   69

Everything Bagel Cauliflower   70

Sexy Salads   **73**

Greek Salad Jar or Bar   74

Fresh Mango Sexy Salad   76

"The More the Miso" Salad Dressing   79

Cowboy Caviar   80

Cobb Salad   83

Fresh Fall Fruity Salad   84

Sweet and Steamy Sexy Salad   87

The "Rachel Green" Salad   88

Sweet Massaged Kale Salad   89

"Oh, Kale Yeah!!" Salad   90

Shira's Fruity Purple Salad   93

Sweet and Crunchy Peanut Salad   94

Fruit and Goat Cheese Salad with a Tangy Vinaigrette   97

Icelandic Beet Carpaccio   98

Dairy-free Caesar   100

Lunches and Dinners   **102**

Ricotta-stuffed Shells   105

California Roll in a Bowl and Miso Soup   106

Meatballs and Dairy-Free Cauli Mash   109

EZ Zucchini Ziti   112

BBQ Lettuce Cups with Avocado   115

Ahi Shawarma Wraps   116

Veggie Fried "Rice" and Seasoned Tofu Steak   118

Easy Roasted Chicken and Eggplant Parmigiana "Noodles"   121

Chicken Chomp   123

Cauliflower Nachos   124

Low Carb Sushi Burrito   127

Beef and Shirataki Noodles   128

Miso Maple Chicken Thighs and Melted Cabbage   131

Power Proteins   **132**

Cloud Bread   **133**

Standard Cloud Bread   134

Cloud Bread Burrito   135

Cloud Bread Cinnamon Rolls   137

Cloud Bread Pizza   138

Avocado Toast   140

Cloud Bread Cinnamon Pancakes   143

PB&J Cloud Bread   144

Everything But the Bagel Cloud Bread   147

Wonder Whips   **149**

OG Peanut Butter Wonder Whip   150

Lemon Blueberry Wonder Whip   153

Birthday "Cake" Wonder Whip   154

Fruity Webble Wonder Whip   157

FroWhoas   **159**

Standard FroWhoa   160

Choczini FroWhoa   161

Choczini Ice Cream   163

Snickers FroWhoa   164

Meat, Chicken & Fish   **166**

Go-to Tuna   167

Silver Egg Salad   169

Meat Lovers Meat   170

Year-Round Instant Pot Turkey Breast   173

Perla's Perfect Salmon   174

Easy Protein Nuggets with Yogurt Dill Sauce   176

Salmon Cakes   177

Supersized Burgers   179

Maple Crusted Air Fried Salmon   180

Crispy Honey Mustard Chicken Nuggets   183

Chicken Marsala   184

Sauces and Dips   **187**

    Pickled Onions   188

    Herb Ranch Dip   189

    Miso Ginger Dip   189

    Sweet Balsamic "Special Sauce"   190

    Maple Tahini Dip   190

    Maple Tahini Salad Dressing   191

    Spicy Mayo   191

    High Protein French Onion Dip   193

    Bangin' Baba Ganoush   194

    Best Sweet Tahini Dressing   195

Savvy Sweets   **196**

    Cottage Cheese Strawberry Ice Cream   197

    Watermelon Cake   199

    Allergy-Friendly Chocolate Discs   200

    chocolate peanut butter mug cake   203

    Nice Cream   204

    Chocolate Coconut Dream Pie   206

    Little Ruthie's Mini Blueberry Muffins   209

    Sour Candy Grape Sticks   210

    Mimi's Easy Yummy Pie   213

Acknowledgements   **214**

About the Author   **216**

Index   **218**

INTRODUCTION

Hi and welcome to the start of your healthy food journey, where you're going to learn to fall in love with the foods that truly love you back. I am so excited as this has been years in the making. Ever since I was a kid, I have loved food. But sadly, my relationship with it was unhealthy and food became an outlet for a lot of unmanaged trauma, boredom, and emotional distress. Thankfully, I've been able to come out of that very dark place and celebrate my love for food via healthful recipes that taste amazing and make me feel my absolute best.

When I was younger and struggling with my weight, my parents struggled with theirs as well. I'll never forget my father telling me, "If it tastes good, it means it's not good for you." While I love my dad and he's right about a lot of things, he was very wrong about this. Once I discovered secret ingredients, devices, cooking methods, and hacks to make healthy food taste delicious, my weight changed for the better, along with my whole relationship with food. Fortunately, so did my dad's.

I learned that you could *Eat Smarter, Not Less*™ to lose weight and started seeing improvements to my health right away. I was so satisfied with my newfound energy and confidence; I knew I wanted to help other people improve their nutrition as well. I became a registered dietitian nutritionist, earned my master's degree in nutrition, and began leading weight loss seminars at UCLA.

Counseling diverse populations gave me the opportunity to understand everyone's favorite comfort foods and which healthy choices were easiest for people to make. Along the way, I've been sharing my easy, healthy, and delicious recipes with my social media following of over three million people who have been asking me to publish this book forever!

I apologize for taking so long, but I've been quite busy. Over the last ten years, I have had three kids and have expanded my nutrition practice to include a digital weight loss program, the 2B Mindset®, Ilana Meals delivery service, and Ilana Housewares, which you will see featured throughout this book.

The mission of this book is to show you how to enjoy your favorite foods and flavors while improving your eating and mindset along the way. I've had so many clients tell me, "Oh, Ilana, I don't need a creamy salad dressing, I'm okay with just sticking to plain lemon juice and olive oil." No offense to plain lemon juice and olive oil, but as I always tell these clients, *We don't need to eat veggies we can 'tolerate,' we need to eat veggies that we crave!* Learning to love veggies and nutritious foods is critical for sustaining a healthy and happy lifestyle. The purpose of this book is to give you healthy recipes that taste like true comfort food, recipes you'll love making and eating for many years to come!

In today's society, we are constantly served copious amounts of carbohydrates. Whenever we go to a restaurant, work meeting, party, or friend's house, we are typically confronted with meals containing lots of bread, pasta, and starches. Those are delicious foods many of us crave, and I explain how to enjoy them within my weight loss program, the 2B Mindset®; but I wanted to highlight more veggie- and protein-packed recipes in this book, because they're my favorite functional foods to focus on. Protein- and veggie-rich foods are also among the foods commonly ignored in today's typical American diet. Veggies and proteins are wellness powerhouses packed with the vitamins, minerals, and amino acids we need to thrive, so don't be surprised if your health and labs improve as a result of eating more of them.

Food influences every cell and process of your body. Every bite of food you eat can either hurt or help benefit your gene expression, microbiome, longevity, brain chemistry, and hormones. With this book, I want you to fall in love with the foods that genuinely love you and your body back.

This is not intended to be a weight loss book by any means. If you want that, be sure to read *You Can Drop It!*, my first book. While you may lose weight and improve your energy and relationship with food with these recipes, this book is not meant to be prescriptive. It is meant rather to inspire you to get creative in the kitchen and explore new varieties of veggies and healthful ingredients that will satisfy your tastebuds and make you feel amazing! A wide range of serving size suggestions are included because we all have different body types, activity levels, physical goals, and needs.

To better keep track of your portions, I recommend ilanahousewares.com for glasses, plates, and bowls intentionally designed for mindful consumption. The whole collection ensures you are more aware of balanced serving sizes in a really chic and sophisticated way.

If you are still hungry after any of the meal suggestions in the book, eat more! That is what the craveable veggies and power proteins are for. If you want a clearer guide on what to eat when you're still hungry, you can follow my "More? Sure!" Model. Start with 16 oz. (500ml) of water first, and make your next bite a serving of veggies to help you fill up smart. Then, if you're still hungry, choose a protein before reaching for carbs to support you in staying fuller longer. For further details on my "More? Sure!" Model, see page 204 of *You Can Drop It!*, and I break these principles down in depth in my 2B Mindset® program if you are curious about learning more.

BREAKFAST

CHOCOLATE CREAM ROLLS

Serves 2

2 bananas

4 eggs

1 tsp. vanilla extract

1½ cups plain Greek yogurt (nonfat or 2 percent) or dairy-free "Greek style" yogurt

1 tbsp. cocoa powder

Pinch of salt

1 tbsp. honey, maple syrup, or monk fruit (or use stevia drops to taste)

Directions

1. Preheat oven to 350 F. Cover a rimmed baking sheet or rectangle cooking dish with parchment paper and spray with oil.

2. Blend bananas, eggs, and vanilla extract in a blender. Pour batter on to the baking sheet and bake for 25 minutes.

3. In the meantime, whip the yogurt with the cocoa powder, salt, and sweetener of choice in a bowl and set aside.

4. Allow the sheet pan banana "cake" to cool. When cooled, spread the yogurt topping evenly over the sheet pan. Slice lengthwise down the center and roll. Serve along with berries and enjoy.

Note: Stores well covered in the refrigerator, so you can prep the recipe in advance and enjoy the second serving on the next day.

PROTEIN OATS

Serves 1–2

1 cup rolled oats

⅓ cup milk

⅓ cup egg whites

1 tbsp. brown sugar

Directions

1. In a small pot on medium-low heat, add your oats and milk. Cook for 5 to 7 minutes or until soft.

2. Once cooked, take off the heat and stir in the brown sugar and egg whites until cooked through with no liquid present.

3. Add your favorite toppings and enjoy a quick and high protein breakfast!

Love the Food that Loves You Back

TEMPEH BLT

Serves 1

1 tsp. avocado or olive oil

3 oz. of smoked tempeh

1 leaf of lettuce

2 slices of tomato

1 English muffin

1 tsp. mayo

Salt and pepper

Directions

1. To a pan on medium-high heat, add the oil.

2. Slice your tempeh and sear each side for 1 to 2 mins.

3. Cut your lettuce and tomato into thick slices.

4. Toast your English muffin and add remaining toppings. Enjoy!

SUPERSIZED SCRAMBLED EGGS AND TOAST

Serves 1

1 egg

2 egg whites

¼ cup low-fat cottage cheese

1 cup veggies, like onions, mushrooms, or bell peppers (optional)

1 tsp. butter, ghee, olive oil, or coconut oil

1 whole wheat English muffin or 1-2 slices of whole wheat sourdough

1 tsp. chives

¼ tsp. red chili flakes

Directions

1. In a mixing bowl, whisk egg, egg whites, cottage cheese, and optional veggies together.

2. Heat a pan with the butter, ghee, or oil.

3. Add the egg mixture and stir often with a spatula for 2 to 5 minutes.

4. Toast your bread.

5. Add cooked eggs and top with chives and red pepper flakes.

6. Serve with additional veggies like sliced tomatoes and enjoy.

Love the Food that Loves You Back

VEGGIE OMELET LOAF

Serves 2

5 eggs

⅓ cup milk of choice

1 medium potato

1 handful of spinach

½–¾ cup grated carrots

1 medium bell
  pepper, diced

½ tsp. baking powder

Salt and pepper

½ cup part-
  skim mozzarella

Directions

1. Preheat the oven to 400 F. Spray a loaf pan with nonstick spray. To make sure there's no sticking and for improved presentation, line the loaf pan with a sheet of parchment paper.

2. In a mixing bowl, add all the ingredients (except mozzarella cheese) and whisk well.

3. Pour into the loaf pan, top with cheese, and bake uncovered for 30 minutes or until the eggs have set.

FRENCH TOAST

Serves 2-3

½ cup egg whites

¼ cup milk

1 large egg

4–6 pieces of light whole wheat or sprouted bread

1 tsp. cinnamon

Sprinkle of powdered sugar (optional)

Directions

1. Heat a large pan on medium high heat.

2. In a bowl, whisk your egg whites, milk, and whole egg. Add your bread and soak each side in the egg/milk mixture for 10 to 15 seconds or until thoroughly soaked.

3. Add your bread to the pan and fry for 2 to 3 minutes on each side or until golden brown.

4. Add cinnamon and powdered sugar, if desired.

Note: Serve with an additional ¼ cup vanilla Greek yogurt for an added boost of protein.

CHOCOLATE CHIP BREAKFAST CAKE

Serves 5–6

3 cups cottage cheese

1 cup egg whites

2 tsps. vanilla extract

1 tsp. liquid stevia or monk fruit

1½ cups whole wheat or gluten free flour

½ cup coconut flour

1½ tsps. baking soda

2 tbsps. brown sugar

¼ cup mini dark chocolate chips

Directions

1. Preheat oven to 350 F.

2. Add all of your wet ingredients to a blender. Blend until smooth. Then add your wet mixture to a bowl.

3. Fold in your flours, baking soda, brown sugar, and chocolate chips.

4. Bake for 35 minutes. Let cool before serving and enjoy.

Note: This is a great recipe to meal prep for breakfasts later in the week.

SEASONAL BREAKFAST BOATS: PAPAYA & SWEET POTATO

Serves 2

1 whole papaya

1½ cups plain or vanilla Greek yogurt or cottage cheese (nonfat or 2 percent)

Kiwi, strawberries, and other berries

2 tbsps. chia seeds

1 tbsp. crushed nuts (optional)

1 tbsp. honey, to drizzle (optional)

Directions

1. Cut the papaya in half, then scoop out the seeds and fleshy bits.

2. Add your yogurt, fruit, and additional toppings. Enjoy!

Alternative:

Replace the papaya with a baked sweet potato. Bake the sweet potato by preheating your oven to 425 F. Wash the sweet potato well and poke holes in it with a fork. Wrap in tin foil or place on a baking sheet and bake for 45 to 50 minutes. You can prepare several of these sweet potatoes in advance.

CRAVEABLE VEGGIES

PASTA SWAPS

We all know that pasta is pasta and there's no true replacement for it, but honestly, these "pasta swaps" are incredible. First off, many of them are even faster than pasta to prepare, like zucchini noodles that can be made into ribbons with a simple veggie peeler and then placed in a pan for only a minute or two to soften.

Second, these veggie pasta swaps don't just taste great, they also make you feel amazing. If you're a volume eater like me, then you know how exhausted you can feel after eating too much spaghetti. However, when it comes to spaghetti squash and other veggie pastas, you actually feel energized after eating a satisfying quantity. And yes, they're so low in calories and high in nutrients like fiber, potassium, and vitamin C that you could (and should) enjoy eating plenty of these wonderful foods. So, while you'll likely still enjoy traditional pasta every once in a while, I hope these recipes inspire you to incorporate more veggies into your daily routine.

THAI PEANUT HEARTS OF PALM SPAGHETTI

Serves 2–4

3 14-oz. cans (1200g) hearts of palm spaghetti, drained and rinsed well

¼ cup (60ml) smooth all-natural peanut butter

¼ cup (60ml) coconut aminos or low sodium soy sauce

1 tbsp. (15ml) rice wine vinegar

1 tsp. (5ml) toasted sesame oil

2 garlic cloves, minced, or 2 frozen garlic cubes

¼ tsp. (1.25g) ground ginger powder or ½ tsp. (2g) grated ginger zest

Garnish

1 tsp. (1.5g) chili flakes or 1 tbsp. (15ml) chili sauce

2 tsps. (8g) peanuts, chopped

1 tbsp. (3g) scallions, chopped

Directions

1. Heat a nonstick pan to medium heat, then add in hearts of palm spaghetti and stir until it is heated through and excess liquid has fully evaporated.

2. In a separate bowl, mix together peanut butter, coconut aminos, rice wine vinegar, sesame oil, garlic, and ginger.

3. Pour the sauce over the hearts of palm spaghetti and mix well.

4. Garnish evenly with chili flakes or sauce, peanuts, and scallions.

THREE WAYS TO COOK SPAGHETTI SQUASH WHOLE

Recipe note: Each of these methods shows you an option for how you can cook spaghetti squash whole. It is a very hard and dangerous vegetable to cut raw because the knife could slip accidentally. Slicing it raw also takes more time, and #NobodyGotTimeForThat.

Oven, my personal favorite:

· Preheat oven to 375 F (190 C). Carefully pierce spaghetti squash all over with a sharp knife or fork and place in an oven-safe cooking dish. Bake for 45 minutes to 90 minutes depending on its size, turning 180 degrees when it is halfway cooked.

· A small 2-pound (900g) squash may take closer to 45 minutes, while a larger, 6-pound (2,720g) spaghetti squash may take closer to 90 minutes to bake.

· When cooled, slice in half. Remove and discard or repurpose the seeds. Use a fork to shred and scoop out the spaghetti squash strands.

Pressure Cooker:

· Carefully pierce spaghetti squash all over with a sharp knife or fork and place spaghetti squash whole in a pressure cooker with ½ cup of water (237ml).

· Cook on high pressure for 15 minutes and release the pressure when finished.

· When cooled, check that the squash is evenly soft. Slice in half. Remove and discard, roast, or plant the seeds. Use a fork to shred and scoop out the spaghetti squash strands.

Love the Food that Loves You Back

Microwave:

- Place the whole spaghetti squash in the microwave and cook on high for 3 minutes or until it is soft enough to slice in half. Slice in half. Remove and discard, roast, or plant the seeds. Cook both spaghetti squash halves in the microwave for an additional 6 to 8 minutes, or until you can easily use a fork to shred and scoop out the spaghetti squash strands.

Note: Always use appliances according to manufacturer's instructions for maximum safety.

SPAGHETTI SQUASH CACIO E PEPI

Serves 2–4

6 cups (1,420ml) cooked spaghetti squash

¼-½ cup (60–120ml) aquafaba, the reserved liquid from a can of chickpeas (a.k.a. garbanzo beans) *or* a cornstarch slurry made by mixing 4 tbsps. (60ml) cold water with 2 tbsps. (20g) cornstarch

½ cup (50g) Parmesan cheese, grated

½ tsp. (1g) black pepper

Directions

1. Toast black pepper in a large saucepan over low to medium heat for 1 to 2 minutes, or until fragrant.

2. Add parmesan cheese and aquafaba or cornstarch slurry to the large saucepan and stir vigorously until well combined.

3. Once evenly mixed into a thick sauce, add in your spaghetti squash.

4. Stir continuously until it's evenly mixed.

5. Garnish with fresh basil (optional).

Note: Liquid from the can of chickpeas is called "aquafaba." It is an alternative thickener for the sauce because we're not using pasta water. You can save and store the chickpeas to add to a sexy salad or use them to make the shakshuka or hummus recipes.

EGGPLANT SESAME NOODLES

Serves 2-4

My thanks to Balle Hurns for this delicious recipe!

Avocado oil or
  coconut oil spray

2 large eggplants, peeled
  and sliced into long
  thin spears

3 large garlic
  cloves, minced

1 tbsp. (15ml) sesame oil

1 tbsp. (15ml) soy sauce

1 tbsp. (15ml) coconut
  aminos or low
  sodium soy sauce

1 tbsp. (13g) brown sugar
  or coconut sugar

¼ cup (25g) scallions,
  chopped, for garnish
  (optional)

1 tbsp. (9g) sesame seeds
  for garnish (optional)

Directions

1. Start by peeling 2 large eggplants and slicing them into ¼-inch thick sticks (about 0.6cm thick).

2. Over medium heat, spray oil, then add eggplant sticks. Cook for 5 to 7 minutes or until soft and flexible; eggplants sticks should be similar in consistency to a cooked, thick udon noodle.

3. Add chopped garlic to a small bowl with sesame oil, soy sauce, coconut aminos or soy sauce, and brown or coconut sugar.

4. Add sauce mixture to eggplant and sauté for an additional 2 to 3 minutes.

5. Add to a bowl and top with scallions, sesame seeds, and chili flakes (optional).

PESTO SHIRATAKI NOODLES

Serves 2-4

4 8-ounce (4 x 225g) bags
  shirataki noodles

6 cups (138g) fresh
  basil, packed

4 cloves garlic

½ cup (25g) Pecorino
  Romano cheese, grated,
  or substitute ⅓ cup (50g)
  nutritional yeast as a
  plant-based alternative

3 tbsps. (45ml) olive oil

3 tbsps. (45ml)
  lemon juice

1 small shallot

¼ cup (32g) walnuts

⅓ cup (~50) chives

¼ (1.4g) tsp. kosher salt

½ cup (120ml) water

Directions

1. Drain and rinse the shirataki noodles.

2. Heat a pan over low to medium heat, add the wet shirataki noodles, and stir for 5 to 10 minutes or until all the water in the noodles has dried out and evaporated.

3. Meanwhile, add all of the remaining ingredients to a blender and pulse until desired consistency is reached.

4. Once the noodles are dry, add the prepared pesto to the noodles and stir to combine. Heat through, about 1 to 2 minutes.

5. Garnish with fresh sliced cherry tomatoes or chili flakes (optional).

6. Top with fresh basil (optional).

FETA PASTA
WITH KELP NOODLES

Serves 2–4

2 12-ounce bags
(680g) kelp noodles
like the kind by Sea
Tangle, drained

1 tsp. (6g) baking soda

6–8 oz. (170–225g) block
feta cheese

8 cloves of garlic

1 tbsp. (15ml) olive oil

2 pints cherry tomatoes
(16 to 24 oz./454–680g),
about 2½ cups (~590ml)

½ tsp. (0.8g) chili flakes

½ tsp. (0.5g) dried oregano

½ cup (10g) fresh
basil leaves

Directions

1. Preheat the oven to 400 F (205 C).

2. Add a block of feta to the center of a baking
   dish, then add cherry tomatoes to surround it.

3. Drizzle with olive oil and sprinkle chili flakes
   and oregano over feta and cherry tomatoes.

4. Bake for 35 minutes or until cherry tomatoes
   soften and start to burst.

5. Meanwhile, fill a large pot with water and
   bring to a boil.

6. Add baking soda and drained kelp noodles to
   boiling water.

7. Boil the noodles until they feel soft and
   flexible when you lift them from the water,
   about 5 minutes. If the kelp noodles feel too
   firm, add an additional ½ tsp. (3g) of baking
   soda. It helps break down the kelp so it is less
   rubbery in texture and more like buttery soft,
   slurpable noodles.

8. Drain and rinse the noodles well to remove
   the baking soda. You should have super
   tender, neutral tasting pasta.

9. Carefully remove the feta and tomatoes
   from the oven. Using the back of a large fork,
   carefully smash the cherry tomatoes and feta
   and stir to combine into a sauce.

10. Add the kelp noodles and mix very well. Top with fresh basil.

Notes: Add ¼ to ½ cup (35–70g) diced cooked chicken or tofu to boost the protein and make the meal extra satisfying.

You can replace kelp noodles with spaghetti squash or hearts of palm pasta if preferred. If using hearts of palm pasta, drain three to four 14-ounce cans (1200g) hearts of palm spaghetti and rinse well with water. To remove the canned taste more, place the hearts of palm noodles in a bowl with ½–1 cup (120–235ml) of dairy milk or almond milk, soak the noodles for 3 to 5 minutes, and rinse well.

ROASTED WONDERS

These roasted veggie wonders are the best when you want something hot, crispy, and comforting. I'm one of those people who is always cold. So even in the spring, you could find me in a fleece sweatshirt and furry boots with a hot cup of tea in my hands. That's why on some days, a cold salad won't cut it, and I run to my oven to roast up these wonders that are delicious to devour when they're hot and steamy. They are so comforting! Feel free to use these roasted veggies as snacks or side dishes, in omelets, as garnishes to soup, or even mixed into salads to give them depth.

EGGPLANT PARM FRIES

Serves 2-4

2 eggplants, cut into fry-like shapes

Olive oil spray

½ cup (65g) of 100 percent whole wheat flour

3 raw eggs

½ tsp. (2.8g) salt

½ tsp. (1g) pepper

½ tsp. (1g) paprika

½ tsp. (1.2g) onion powder

½ tsp. (0.8g) garlic powder

Directions

1. Preheat oven to 375 degrees F (190 C).

2. Prepare a sheet pan with parchment paper and coat with oil spray.

3. Slice an eggplant into fry shapes; set aside.

4. To a large bowl, add about ½ cup (65g) 100 percent whole wheat flour (you can swap for a gluten free flour if needed).

5. Add 3 raw eggs to the large bowl.

6. Season with salt, pepper, onion powder, garlic powder, and paprika.

7. Prepare another large bowl with seasoned whole wheat breadcrumbs. (Optional to add parmesan cheese.)

8. Work in batches, coating the eggplant first in flour, then in egg, then in breadcrumbs.

9. Place eggplant fries on the baking sheet and cook for 25 min. You can optionally flip them halfway. You could also use an air fryer to cut down the cooking time.

10. Enjoy on their own or dip into marinara.

BROCCOLI CRUNCH WITH RANCH DIP

Serves 2–4

Coconut oil or avocado oil spray

2-pound (900g) bag triple washed raw broccoli florets or 8–10 cups (1,400–1,750g) washed broccoli heads

1 tbsp. (15ml) olive oil

½ tsp. (2.8g) salt

½–1 tsp. (0.8–1.6g) garlic powder

⅓ cup (80ml) high protein plain, unsweetened yogurt or dairy-free substitute

½ tsp. (0.8g) ranch seasoning

1½ tsp. (2g) scallions or chives, chopped

Directions

1. Preheat the oven to 425 F (220 C). Line a baking sheet with parchment paper coated with spray.

2. Add broccoli to the pan and drizzle evenly with olive oil and salt.

3. Massage oil and salt into the broccoli for 2 to 3 minutes. Be sure to give each head of broccoli a good squeeze as it helps get the broccoli extra tender on the inside and crispy on the outside.

4. Spread the broccoli into an even layer on the pan and sprinkle evenly with garlic powder.

5. Roast the broccoli in the oven for 25 minutes, tossing it midway.

6. Increase heat to broil for 2 to 3 minutes for extra crispy broccoli.

7. In a separate bowl, mix together the yogurt, ranch, and scallions to make a dipping sauce for the broccoli.

AIR FRIED MINI BELL PEPPERS

Serves 2–4

2 pounds (~910g) mini
  bell peppers

Olive oil spray

Salt and pepper to taste

Directions

1. Add mini bell peppers to the air fryer

2. Toss with olive oil, salt and pepper

3. Air fry at 400 F (205 C) for 13 minutes, flipping
   halfway through.

Note: This method works perfectly with button or
baby portobello mushrooms as well. Add flaky salt to
garnish once ready to eat.

MUSHROOM CAP PIZZAS

Serves 1–2

2 large mushroom
caps, cleaned

¼ cup (60ml) pizza or
marinara sauce

⅓ cup (45g) part
skim mozzarella
cheese, grated

Garlic powder and red
chili flakes to taste

Additional toppings of
your choice (optional)

Directions

1. Line a baking sheet with parchment paper and spray with oil.

2. Preheat oven to 400 F (205 C)

3. Bake 2 mushroom caps, gills side up, for 5 minutes.

4. Carefully remove the pan from the oven and blot away the excess liquid.

5. Top the mushroom caps evenly with sauce and cheese, then bake for another 10 minutes or until the cheese is bubbly.

Note: Added pepperoni, herbs, and ¼ cup (30g) more cheese for photos.

KOHLRABI NACHOS

Serves 1–2

2 medium kohlrabi

1 tbsp. (10g) cornstarch

1 tsp. (3g) citrus lime seasoning, either Tajín seasoning, the kind by Trader Joe's, or similar

2 tbsps. (28g) mozzarella, shredded

2 tsps. (2.2g) pickled onion

1 tsp. (1g) pickled jalapeño

Optional garnishes: Pico de gallo, red onion, pickled jalapeños, salsa, olives, and fresh cilantro

Directions

1. Wash, peel, and slice kohlrabi into thin chip-like rounds.

2. Preheat air fryer or oven to 400 F (205 C). If using an oven, line a baking sheet with parchment paper and spray with oil. Set aside.

3. In a mixing bowl, toss kohlrabi slices with cornstarch and seasoning.

4. Spray air fryer with oil spray and place the kohlrabi slices evenly on top of the basket. If using an oven, place the kohlrabi slices on the baking sheet. Cook at 400 F (205 C) for 9 minutes in the air fryer or 15 minutes in the oven.

5. Top with cheese, then cook for an additional 2 to 3 minutes or until cheese is bubbly. If using an oven, use the broil setting for 2 minutes for a sizzling cheese layer.

6. Add pickled onions, jalapeños, and optional toppings of your choice and enjoy!

PARM CRUSTED PALM

Serves 1–2

1 14-oz. can hearts of palm (400g), drained

2 tbsps. (15g) whole wheat breadcrumbs or whole wheat panko crumbs

1 tbsp. (8g) whole wheat flour

2 tbsps. (15g) Parmesan cheese

½ tsp. (0.8g) garlic powder

Salt to taste

Oil spray

½ cup (118ml) marinara sauce for dipping (optional)

Directions

1. Preheat the oven to 400 degrees F (205 C).

2. Line a baking sheet with parchment paper and spray with oil.

3. Mix breadcrumbs, flour, parmesan cheese, garlic powder, and salt to make the breadcrumb mixture.

4. Roll the hearts of palm into the breadcrumb mix, pressing down firmly so the breadcrumbs stick. (You may want to dry the hearts of palm off first using a paper towel to help the process.) Place on your baking sheet.

5. Spray the tops of the hearts of palm with oil spray and bake for 20 to 30 minutes. I broiled them for another 2 to 3 minutes at the end to get them extra crispy.

6. Then dip in marinara and enjoy!

BASKET OF FRIES

Serves 1–2

2 medium turnips,
  rutabagas, or celery root

1 tsp. (5ml) olive oil

Olive oil spray

¼ tsp. (1.4g) salt

½ tsp. (0.8g) garlic powder

¼ tsp. (0.7g) cumin

Directions

1. Wash and clean root vegetables. If using celery root, peel the exterior.

2. Cut veggies into fry-like shapes.

3. Toss vegetables with olive oil and salt.

4. Air fry for 15 minutes at 400 F (205 C). If using an oven, line a baking sheet with parchment paper and spray with oil, then bake at 400 F (205 C) for 25 to 30 minutes, flipping once halfway through.

Note: Feel free to swap out salt, garlic, and cumin for ranch seasoning, BBQ rub mix, za'atar, everything bagel seasoning, shawarma spice, or truffle salt.

CAULIFLOWER TOASTS

Serves 2-4

18–24 oz. (510–680g)
  frozen cauliflower rice

1 large egg

1 tbsp. (15g)
  Parmesan cheese

¼ tsp. (1.4g) salt

**To make savory
  toasts, add:**

¼ tsp. (0.4g) garlic powder

¼ tsp. (0.3g) oregano

Directions

1. Steam or microwave frozen cauliflower rice for 4 to 6 minutes. Let cool.

2. Use a cheesecloth or dish towel to squeeze out all of the liquid.

3. To a bowl, add 1 egg, cheese, salt, and seasonings, if using.

4. Flatten the mix into squares, circles, or whatever shapes you prefer. Place on a baking sheet lined with wax paper or parchment paper sprayed with nonstick spray.

5. Bake at 375 F (190 C) for 20 to 25 minutes, depending on how soft or firm you want them.

Notes: To freeze, just use wax or parchment paper sheets in between each one and stack in an airtight container. You can heat them back up in a skillet whenever you're ready.

These are delicious when made savory, but you might want to keep them plain if you plan to top them with sweeter items like nut butter or cream cheese and jam.

MAPLE BACON BRUSSELS SPROUTS

Serves 2–4

1¼ lbs. (570g) raw brussels sprouts, stems removed

3 tbsps. balsamic vinegar

2 tbsps. (30ml) extra-virgin olive oil

1½ tbsps. (25ml) maple syrup, monk fruit syrup, or honey

Salt to taste

Pepper to taste

3 slices turkey bacon or vegan bacon alternative

Directions

1. Add water to a medium pot and bring to a boil.

2. Preheat oven to 400 F (205 C). Line a baking sheet with parchment paper and spray with oil. Set aside.

3. Place raw brussels sprouts in the pot in boiling water for 5 to 10 minutes. When almost tender, drain and set aside to cool.

4. In a small bowl, mix balsamic vinegar, olive oil, syrup or honey, and pinches of salt and pepper. When brussels sprouts have cooled, cut them in half and toss with dressing.

5. Place on the baking sheet and bake in the oven for 15 minutes.

6. While sprouts are baking, cut turkey bacon into small pieces and cook in a hot pan till crispy.

7. Serve sprouts with bacon bits. Enjoy.

Love the Food that Loves You Back

EVERYTHING EGGPLANT "TACOS" AND MINI TORTILLAS

Serves 1-2

Avocado oil, coconut oil, or olive oil spray

½ tsp. (1.6g) "everything" bagel seasoning

1 large globe eggplant, sliced into ½-inch thick rounds (1.3cm thick)

Directions

1. Preheat oven to 375 F (190 C).

2. Slice eggplant thin. Spray with oil on both sides and sprinkle with seasoned salt.

3. Bake on a baking sheet for 25 to 30 minutes.

Notes: To make eggplant "tacos" as in the image, cut the eggplant lengthwise to make more room for toppings. You can also use slightly less toppings and roll up the eggplant to get your fillings tight in a bundle.

To make them more like mini "tortillas," cut the eggplant into circles. Get creative! I love to use eggplant to make sandwiches with sliced chicken breast, hot sauce, and shredded greens. I'm excited to see what you come up with.

TAHINI TERIYAKI ROASTED CARROTS

Serves 2–4

8 whole carrots, peeled

2 tsp. (10g) coconut oil or avocado oil

1½ tbsps. (23g) tahini

1½ tbsps. (23ml) water

1½ tbsps. (23ml) teriyaki sauce

¼ cup (44g) pomegranate seeds

Directions

1. Preheat the oven to 425 F (220 C). Line a baking sheet with parchment paper.

2. Rub whole carrots with oil and place on the baking sheet. Bake for 15 minutes; carefully remove from the oven to flip carrots over. Bake for an additional 15 to 20 minutes or until you can easily insert a fork.

3. In a small bowl, whisk tahini with water and set aside to thicken.

4. Remove carrots from the oven and place on a serving plate. Drizzle with tahini and teriyaki. Top with pomegranate seeds.

LEVELED UP SHISHITO PEPPERS

Serves 2–4

1 small (approx. 10-oz./300ml) can mandarin oranges, packed in juice not syrup, or 2 fresh mandarin oranges, peeled

5–6 cups (590–710g) shishito peppers

2 tbsps. (30ml) champagne vinegar

2 tbsps. (30ml) olive oil

1 tbsp. (15ml) lemon juice

1 tbsp. (9g) Tajín or chili citrus seasoning

¼ cup (30g) pepitas or pumpkin seeds

2 tbsps. (4g) fresh mint leaves, chopped

2 tbsps. (6g) fresh cilantro, chopped

2 tbsps. (8g) fresh parsley, chopped (optional)

Directions

1. Preheat the oven to 400 F (205 C). Line a baking sheet with parchment paper and spray with oil. Add pepitas to the baking sheet, then spread half the Tajín seasoning all over the pepitas. Toss with a spoon and add the rest of the seasoning on top. Bake for 5 minutes or until fragrant. Set aside and let cool.

2. On a separate baking sheet lined with parchment paper, add the shishito peppers; spray with oil and cook for 9 to 12 minutes, tossing halfway through.

3. In an air fryer: Cook shishito peppers at 400 F (205 C) until blistered, about 8 to 9 minutes.

To make the dressing: In a small bowl, whisk vinegar, olive oil, and lemon juice together. If using canned mandarin oranges, add 1 tablespoon of the juice from the can. If using fresh, use the juice from ½ mandarin orange. Toss blistered shishito peppers with vinaigrette. Top with Tajín-toasted pepitas and remaining mandarin orange slices.

ILANA MEALS
BLISTERED VEGGIES

Serves 1–2

1.5 tbsps. (23ml) olive oil

1 cup (125g) green beans

¼ cup (25g) red
  onions, rough cut

¼ cup (45g) yellow bell
  peppers, rough cut

¼ cup (45g) red bell
  peppers, rough cut

1 tsp. (5.7g) kosher salt

1 tsp. (2.3g) black pepper

Directions

1. In a sauté pan, heat olive oil on high heat.

2. Add green beans, onions, and bell peppers,
    and sauté until vegetables begin to blister
    and soften.

3. Season with salt and pepper.

EVERYTHING BAGEL CAULIFLOWER

Serves 2–4

1 cauliflower head, with leaves removed but head intact

½ cup (120ml) vegan sour cream or reduced fat sour cream

1 tbsp. (8g) "everything" bagel seasoning

2 cloves of garlic, crushed

Directions

1. Fill a large pot with water and bring to a boil over medium heat.

2. Meanwhile, soak the head of cauliflower in a bowl of water with a teaspoon (5ml) white vinegar or apple cider vinegar to clean it and remove any dirt or bugs.

3. Line a baking sheet with parchment paper and set aside and preheat the oven to 400 F (205 C).

4. Carefully submerge the head of cauliflower in the boiling water for five to seven minutes or until a fork easily pierces through the stem. You want it to be tender but remain intact.

5. While the water is boiling, prepare the spread by mixing the everything bagel seasoning and crushed garlic with the sour cream until well combined.

6. Carefully remove the cauliflower from the pot of water and place on the baking sheet; let cool.

7. Using clean hands or gloves, spread the cream mixture all over the cauliflower head, making sure to get it into the grooves of the florets so that every piece is smothered.

8. Place the baking sheet in the oven and bake for 15 minutes, letting the cream dry up and soak into the cauliflower.

9. Turn the oven to broil for 2 to 5 minutes, until the top of the cauliflower head is toasted, not burned.

10. Garnish with chopped chives or parsley (optional).

Note: Triple this recipe to make in advance for meals, a potluck, or to serve to friends and family. Everyone loves it!

SAD SALAD   VS.   SEXY SALAD

SEXY SALAD IN 6 STEPS

Step 1: Red 💋   **Step 2: Orange** 🔥   **Step 3: Yellow** ⚡

@ilanamuhlsteinrd

Step 4: Green 🌴   **Step 5: Purple** 🦄   **Step 6: Protein** 💪

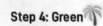
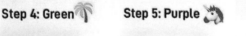

SEXY SALADS

I started using the term "sexy salads" almost ten years ago. In fact, defining a "sexy salad" was the topic of one of the first videos I ever posted on social media back in 2016. In that video, I explain that when I describe a dish as a "sexy salad," it means that it has every color of the rainbow in it. I even created infographics showing the colors: Red could be tomatoes, strawberries, bell peppers, and radishes. Orange could be roasted butternut squash and carrots. Yellow can be represented with bell peppers, onion, yellow beets. Greens are easy, because aside from lettuce, you have fennel, broccoli, celery, okra, bok choy, and so much more. Lastly, for blue/purple, you can use blueberries, red onion, purple cabbage, and dark radicchio. As I created dozens of sexy salad creations in that era, I realized that it is more than just the visual color scheme that makes a salad scrumptious or "sexy." It's the dynamic blend of flavors, textures, temperatures, and shapes. I've loosened up the criteria in the last few years to include any salad that satisfies you and becomes something you actually crave.

When you get to that place in your health and wellness journey, I find that your mindset toward food becomes very freeing and positive. It has made a massive improvement to my entire life—mind, body, and soul—and has even helped with my health during my pregnancies (as pictured here circa 2018, when I was pregnant with my second child, Julian).

All of these recipes are designed to be played with. Feel free to add proteins like sliced chicken, tofu, or cottage cheese when you like. You can add more tasty toppings like feta cheese or avocado if you want to make it more decadent. And of course, have fun varying the type of lettuce and veggies you use based on what is in season and available to you. Just promise me one thing: if you post your sexy salad online, use the hashtag #IlanasSexySalads, which has been going strong with yummy salad inspo since 2015.

GREEK SALAD JAR OR BAR

Serves 2–4

Dressing

¼ cup (60ml) red
wine vinegar

2 tbsps. (30ml) olive oil

½ tsp. (2.8g) salt

½ tsp. (0.5g) dried oregano

¼ tsp. (0.6g) pepper

1 tsp. (5g) Dijon mustard

1 tsp. (5ml) agave syrup,
honey, or maple syrup

Salad

2 heads romaine
lettuce, washed, dried,
and chopped

1 green bell
pepper, chopped

4 oz. (115g) block
feta cheese

2 Roma tomatoes,
chopped, or 1½
cups (225g) cherry
tomatoes, sliced

½ English
cucumber, chopped

2 tbsps. (23g) black
olives, chopped

2 tbsps. (15g) crushed
walnuts (optional)

Equipment

2 32-ounce or 4 16-ounce
Mason jars or similar
canning jars (four 500ml
Mason jars or two 1-liter
canning jars)

Directions

1. In a bowl, whisk together dressing ingredients. Divide equally to fill the bottom of two 32-ouncee (two 1-liter jars) or four 16-ouncee Mason jars (four 500-ml jars).

2. Begin to fill each jar with equal amounts of onions or shallots, if using. They will soak up the vinegar mix and become part of the dressing.

3. Continue to layer the salad jars by adding equal amounts of the peppers, then lettuce, followed by the feta, tomatoes, cucumber, olives, and walnuts, if using.

4. When ready to eat:

    a. Open the jar and place the open end of the plate on top of the opening of the jar. It should look like the jar is wearing the plate as a hat.

    b. Press on the plate so that it stays connected to the jar while you flip it over.

    c. Slowly lift the jar so that the salad pours out and begins to fill the plate.

    d. The salad dressing mixture should come out last and dress the vegetables beneath it. Toss lightly and enjoy.

You can also mix this salad together without the jar using a traditional salad bowl, or you can serve it for guests to set up their own salad jars by keeping each ingredient separated in small bowls so people can build it on their own. Be sure to let the onions soak in the vinaigrette for at least 30 minutes in a separate bowl prior to serving. You can make this without the romaine lettuce and double or triple the number of cucumbers instead.

FRESH MANGO SEXY SALAD

Serves 4–6

Dressing

¼ cup (60ml) olive oil

1½ tbsps. (22ml) red
   wine vinegar

3 tbsps. (44ml) lime juice

2 tbsps. (42g) honey

1 tsp. (0.7g) dried basil

½ tsp. (0.8g) garlic powder

½ tsp. (1.2g) onion powder

½ tsp. (2.8g) salt

Pinch black pepper

Salad

4 cups (220g) chopped
   romaine lettuce

2 cups (300g)
   cucumber, chopped

1 red bell pepper

1 cup (165g)
   mango, chopped

½ red onion, chopped

½ cup (65g) toasted or raw
   sunflower seeds

Directions

1. Mix salad dressing ingredients together in a
    large salad bowl.

2. Add salad ingredients on top of the dressing
    and mix it all together.

"THE MORE THE MISO" SALAD DRESSING

Serves 6–8

Sesame Ginger Dressing

½ cup (120ml) rice wine vinegar

1 tbsp. (15ml) sesame oil

1 tbsp. (15ml) olive or grapeseed oil

3 tbsps. (45ml) water

2 tsps. (10g) miso paste

2 whole carrots, peeled and chopped

⅛ onion, chopped

1¼ inch ginger root

1 tbsp. honey (21g) or 1–2 stevia packets

Pinch of salt or 1 tsp. (5ml) low sodium soy sauce to taste

Directions

1. Make the dressing by blending together all the sesame ginger dressing ingredients except the salt and soy sauce.

2. Add salt or soy sauce to taste. Makes about one cup dressing (237ml).

3. Use the dressing to top your favorite salad ingredients, such as romaine or spinach leaves, cucumbers, sugar snap peas, red bell peppers, and mandarin oranges.

4. This dressing also pairs well with raw tofu and roasted veggies.

COWBOY CAVIAR

Serves 4–8

2 large tomatoes, diced

2 large cucumbers, diced

1 15-oz. can corn kernels (~350g drained), or the corn sliced from about 2 ears of cooked corn on the cob

1 15-oz. can black beans (~255g drained), rinsed

1 large red onion, diced

⅓ cup (6g) cilantro leaves

½ cup (75g) feta cheese, crumbled

1 jicama or 2 large carrots, diced

Dressing

Juice of 2 limes

2 tbsps. (15g) olive oil

2 tsp. (14g) honey

½ tsp. (2.8g) salt

½ tsp. (1g) pepper

Directions

1. Chop all vegetables into small pieces and add to a large bowl. I highly recommend using a large salad chopper for this recipe if you have one.

2. In a small bowl, mix dressing ingredients together and toss over salad.

3. Enjoy!

Notes: Add chicken or flaked albacore tuna to make this a complete lunch.

You can also leave out the corn and replace it with 1 cup (~30g) of bean based or other high fiber chips to keep the carb content balanced with higher fiber.

COBB SALAD

Serves 2–4

3 heads of romaine lettuce, chopped

½ cup (90g) cherry tomatoes, sliced

3 hard-boiled eggs, sliced

1 cup (150g) sliced grilled chicken breast or 1 cup (240g) extra firm tofu, cubed

2 strips cooked turkey bacon or cooked pastrami, diced

Dressing

3 tbsps. (45g) low-fat or avocado mayonnaise, or full-fat Greek yogurt

1 tbsp. (15g) Dijon mustard

1 tbsp. (15ml) apple cider vinegar

½ lemon

1 tsp. (5ml) Worcestershire

2 garlic cloves, crushed (or use 2 frozen garlic cubes)

¼ cup (60ml) oil

2 tbsps. (30ml) water

Salt and pepper to taste

Directions

1. Chop all vegetables and add to a large bowl.

2. In a small bowl, mix dressing ingredients together and toss over salad.

3. Enjoy!

Note: This makes a super easy weeknight dinner.

FRESH FALL FRUITY SALAD

(Perfect for Rosh Hashana)
Serves 4–8

Dressing

¼ cup (60ml) rice
  wine vinegar

2 tbsps. (30ml) olive oil

1 tsp. (5ml) low sodium soy
  sauce or coconut aminos

1 tsp. (5ml) honey

½ tsp. (2.8g) salt

½ tsp. (1g) pepper

Salad

6–8 cups (400–540g)
  kale, washed, dried,
  and chopped

1 English cucumber
  or 3–4 Persian
  cucumbers, chopped

½ red onion, chopped

1 medium red
  apple, chopped

½ cup (45g)
  pomegranate seeds

¼ cup (30g) goat cheese
  (optional)

2 tbsps. (15g)
  walnuts, crushed

Directions

1. Whisk together the dressing ingredients in a small bowl and set aside.

2. Add kale to a large salad bowl and massage for a minute or two with your hands to break it down a bit. Pour dressing over kale, then massage again so each piece is well dressed.

3. Add the remaining ingredients and toss.

Notes: This is ideal in the fall when apples and pomegranates are in season, but make it year-round. It's delicious.

You can prepare this salad in jars up to four days in advance by equally distributing the dressing at the bottom of two 32-ounce (two 1-liter) canning jars or four 16-ounce (four 500ml) Mason jars. Add the onion on top of the dressing, followed by the kale, cucumber, pomegranate seeds, apple, goat cheese, and walnuts.

SWEET AND STEAMY SEXY SALAD

Serves 2–4

Dressing

3 tbsps. (45g) tahini

1½ tbsps. (23ml) coconut aminos or low sodium soy sauce

1 tbsp. (15ml) lemon juice

1 tbsp. (20g) silan, a.k.a. date syrup, or 1 tbsp. (15ml) maple syrup

3 tbsps. (45ml) water

Salad

4 cups (350g) shaved brussels sprouts, roughly chopped

4 cups (270g) dinosaur or lacinato kale, with stems removed and chopped

1 tsp. (5ml) olive oil

1 steamed beet, chopped

2 tbsps. (20g) hemp seeds

1 carrot, peeled into strips and chopped, or ½ cup (55g) shredded carrots

Directions

1. Sautee the brussels sprouts and kale in olive oil for 3 to 4 minutes until softened.

2. In a bowl or jar, mix together the first five ingredients to make the dressing.

3. Place the cooked brussels sprouts and kale in a bowl. Top with chopped beets, carrots, and hemp hearts. Add salad dressing and mix well.

Warning: *Very addictive!*

THE "RACHEL GREEN" SALAD

Serves 2–4

¼ cup (60ml) lemon juice

3 tbsps. (45ml) extra-
virgin olive oil

1–2 cloves garlic, grated

¼ tsp. (1.4g) salt

¼ tsp. (0.6g) pepper

1 cup cooked chickpeas
(a.k.a. garbanzo beans),
rinsed and drained

1 red onion, chopped

1 English cucumber
or 4–5 Persian
cucumbers, chopped

2 cups (300g) cherry
tomatoes, sliced

¼ cup (8g) fresh
mint, chopped

¼ cup (16g) fresh
parsley, chopped

⅓ cup (50g) feta
cheese, crumbled

2 tbsps. (20g)
pistachios, chopped

Directions

1. At the bottom of a large salad bowl, whisk together the first five ingredients.

2. Add the remaining ingredients and toss well to combine. (You can prepare this salad in jars up to 4 days in advance for future meals by equally dispersing the dressing at the bottom of two 32-ounce canning jars [2 one-liter jars] or four 16-ounce Mason jars [four 500ml Mason jars].)

3. Add the chickpeas and onions on top of the dressing, followed by the mint, parsley, cucumber, tomatoes, and feta.

SWEET MASSAGED KALE SALAD

Serves 2–4

Juice of two lemons

2 tbsps. (30ml) olive oil

2 tbsps. (30ml)
  maple syrup

½ tsp. (2.8g) salt

Fresh cracked pepper

6–8 cups (400–650g)
  kale, chopped with
  stems removed

¼ cup (50g) cherry
  tomatoes or roasted red
  peppers, sliced

2 tbsps. (15g) toasted
  pumpkin or
  sunflower seeds

2 Persian cucumbers,
  thinly sliced

½ cup (120g) jicama
  or sliced purple
  cabbage, chopped into
  small pieces

This works great as a vegan meal mixed with edamame and a sprinkle of hemp seeds.

Directions

1. Whisk together olive oil, lemon juice, maple syrup, salt, and pepper.

2. Pour dressing onto kale and massage with hands to ensure the kale is well dressed and well wilted.

3. Add cherry tomatoes, cucumbers, and chopped jicama or cabbage for color and crunch.

4. Toss to coat.

"OH, KALE YEAH!!" SALAD

Serves 3-6

6 cups (400g) or one big bag of prewashed curly kale, roughly chopped

1 large ripe avocado

Juice of 1–2 lemons (I like it very lemony)

1 tsp. (5.5g) high-quality sea salt

4–6 dried apricots or one freshly cut persimmon, pear, or red apple, chopped

2 tbsps. (20g) cashews, chopped

½ tsp. (0.8g) red chili flakes (optional)

2 tbsps. (7g) pickled onions (optional)

Directions

1. To a large bowl, add the washed and chopped kale. With clean hands and jewelry removed, add the avocado to the kale; massage it in for two to three minutes with your hands and watch it soften the kale.

2. Squeeze the lemon and sprinkle the salt evenly over the kale; massage for an additional minute. This creates the dressing for the kale.

3. Next, you can add whatever you want. I love adding chopped apricot, nuts, tomatoes, onion, and even more diced avocado. It's delicious, people love it, and it holds up well.

Note: Kale is pretty sturdy, so you can make this 2 to 4 hours before serving and it stays fresh and delicious. Just cover it and keep it in the fridge!

Love the Food that Loves You Back

SHIRA'S FRUITY PURPLE SALAD

Serves 3–6

4 cups thinly sliced purple cabbage or 1 32-ounce bag of shredded purple cabbage (360–900g)

2 cups shredded carrots or 1 16-ounce bag of shredded carrots (220–450g)

8 oz. (225g) fresh blueberries, washed

¼ cup (32g) unsweetened dried cranberries, chopped

2 scallions, chopped

¼ cup (20g) slivered almonds, preferably toasted

2 fresh mandarin oranges, peeled and chopped, or 1 can (10 oz./300ml) mandarin orange slices (packed in juice, not syrup), drained but reserve the juice, and chopped

¼ cup (60ml) olive oil

2 tbsps. (30ml) white vinegar

Juice from half a mandarin orange, or 2 tbsps. (30ml) juice from can of mandarin oranges

Juice of one lemon

Salt and pepper to taste

Directions

1. In a large salad bowl, whisk olive oil, white vinegar, squeeze of lemon, salt, and pepper.

2. Add shredded purple cabbage and carrots to the large bowl and toss well.

3. Add blueberries, dried cranberries, oranges, and chopped scallions; toss lightly.

Note: This is wonderful for Mother's Day or any celebratory brunch. It's a crowd-pleaser and looks beautiful on a table.

SWEET AND CRUNCHY PEANUT SALAD

Serves 2–4

Dressing:

¼ cup (60ml) apple cider vinegar

¼ cup (60ml) soy sauce or coconut aminos

¼ cup (60g) peanut butter or sunflower seed butter

2 tbsps. (25g) sugar or honey, or 4 packets stevia or monk fruit

About 2 tbsps. (30ml) warm water to thin out

Salad

6 cups (540–720g) shredded cabbage, brussels sprouts, or bok choy, raw and chopped well

¼ cup (25g) chopped red onion or scallions

2 tbsps. (20g) pomegranate seeds or raisins or dates, chopped

2 tbsps. (20g) peanuts, sunflower seeds, pecans, hemp seeds, or almonds, chopped and slivered

Cherry tomatoes, yellow bell pepper, shredded carrots, and cucumbers, sliced (optional)

Directions

1. Chop salad ingredients and add them to bowl.

2. Mix dressing ingredients in a separate bowl.

3. Pour dressing over salad, toss, and enjoy!

Note: In the summer, I prefer to eat this salad raw and really enjoy the raw bok choy in it. If you'd prefer a more comforting dish for the colder months, you can cut the bok choy in larger pieces lengthwise and pan-sear it with a small amount of olive oil. This adds a lot of flavor and crispness!

FRUIT AND GOAT CHEESE SALAD WITH A TANGY VINAIGRETTE

Serves 2–4

Salad

4–6 cups (120–180g) spinach

¼ cup (45g) goat cheese

¼ cup (8g) fresh mint, chopped

¼ cup (8g) fresh basil, chopped

1 peach, pear, or apple, thinly sliced

2 Persian cucumbers, chopped

¼ red onion, chopped

2 tbsps. (15g) dried unsweetened cranberries, roughly chopped

2 tbsps. (20g) crushed walnuts (optional)

Dressing

2 tbsps. (30ml) balsamic vinegar

1 tbsp. (15ml) rice wine vinegar

2 tbsps. (30ml) olive oil

1 tbsp. (22g) honey

1 tbsp. (15g) Dijon mustard

½ tsp. (2.8g) salt

Directions

1. Chop ingredients and add to a large bowl.

2. In a small bowl, whisk ingredients for dressing, then top salad with dressing. Enjoy!

ICELANDIC BEET CARPACCIO

Serves 2–4

2 large red or yellow beets

2 tbsps. (30g)
 truffle mayonnaise

½ lemon

1½ tbsps. (15g)
 hazelnuts, chopped

1 tbsp. (6g) Parmesan
 cheese, shaved

3–4 cups (120–160g) wild
 greens like arugula

Grated dried mushrooms
 for garnish (optional)

Because there is so much snow on the ground in Iceland, underground root veggies like beets are more accessible and so this salad may as well be their national salad. I looked forward to eating it every day I was there.

Directions

1. Fill a large pot with water and bring to a boil. Add the beets and boil for 25 minutes or until you can easily insert a fork.

2. In a large pan, toast hazelnuts over low heat until fragrant, about 2 to 3 minutes. Remove from heat and set aside to let cool.

3. Drain the beets, and when cooled, rub the beets to remove the peel. You might want to wear gloves as beets can stain your hands for a day or two. The skins should slip off easily under running cold water.

4. Slice beets thin and uniform in size and place in an even layer on a large round plate in the shape of a circle.

5. Drizzle truffle mayo on top of the beet slices. Add arugula and squeeze lemon lightly on top. Top with parmesan cheese and hazelnuts. Serve and enjoy!

DAIRY-FREE CAESAR

Serves 8–12

3 heads romaine lettuce, washed and chopped

1 English cucumber or 3–4 Persian cucumbers, diced

½ red onion or ½ cup (50g) pickled red onions, sliced

1 cup (150g) cherry tomatoes, sliced (optional)

1 cup (145g) hearts of palm, diced (optional)

To Make Croutons

2 slices bread, whole grain, sourdough, or high fiber, sliced into cubes

½ tbsp. (7ml or 7g) olive oil, butter, or ghee

1 clove garlic, crushed, or one frozen garlic cube

Dressing

1 cup (220g) reduced fat or avocado mayo

3 tbsps. (45ml) lemon juice

1 tbsp. (15ml) white vinegar

4 to 5 cloves of garlic

1 tsp. (5g) Dijon mustard

½ tsp. (2.8g) salt

¼ tsp. (0.25g) oregano

⅛ tsp. (0.3g) black pepper

2 tbsps. (30ml) hot water

2¼ tbsps. (24g) nutritional yeast

Directions

1. To make the croutons, toss bread in a bowl with olive oil and seasoning.

2. Preheat a pan or air fryer and spray with oil spray.

3. Add bread to the pan or air fryer and let toast or crisp for 5 to 6 minutes. Set aside.

4. To make single serving salads, plate 2 cups of romaine lettuce per salad with ¼ cup (40g) each tomatoes and cucumbers.

5. Add two tablespoons (20g) of onion and dressing and toss well.

6. Top with 1 to 2 tablespoons of croutons along with grilled chicken or protein of your choice for a complete dinner. If you want to enjoy this salad for lunch, add ½ to ¾ cup (85–125g) chickpeas or any fiber filled carb of your choice.

Note: Dressing is great to make in a large batch and keep up to a week in the refrigerator. This salad also works great for a large party or potluck meal.

LUNCHES AND DINNERS

Here are lots of yummy meals I love eating and sharing with my family and friends. I think you will really enjoy them too. Within my weight loss program, I recommend plating your meals slightly differently at lunch and dinner, but I decided to keep these recipes together for this cookbook because many of the dinner recipes taste wonderful for lunch the next day as well. If you are following my 2B Mindset® nutrition plan, feel free to pair these meals with more fiber filled carbohydrates or craveable veggies when plating these meals at lunch or dinner. Remember to figure out what works best for you and your goals, just try, track, and see.

RICOTTA-STUFFED SHELLS

Serves 4–5

2 cups (240g) part
  skim shredded
  mozzarella, divided

2 cups (473ml) marinara
  sauce, divided

½ cup (50g) Parmesan
  cheese, grated

16 oz. (453g) part skim or
  low-fat ricotta cheese

Whole large cabbage

1 egg

2 tbsps. (12g)
  Italian seasoning

Salt and pepper to taste

I was inspired to make this recipe in an attempt to encourage my husband to eat more cruciferous veggies like broccoli and cauliflower to help lower his cholesterol. We all love stuffed cabbage with meat, so I figured why not stuff them like I would manicotti? What resulted were these delicious Ricotta-Stuffed Shells, and they went instantly viral on social media. They are almost too good to believe you're eating a bunch of cabbage.

Directions

1. Core the cabbage and boil it whole for 20 minutes.

2. Add 1 cup (237ml) marinara sauce to the bottom of a 9-x-13-inch (23-x-33-cm) baking dish.

3. Preheat the oven to 375 F (190 C). Prepare the filling by mixing ricotta with egg, 1½ cups (180g) mozzarella, Italian seasoning, and ¼ cup (25g) Parmesan cheese.

4. Drain the cabbage well and peel off the leaves.

5. Using 2 to 3 leaves at a time, add 2 to 4 tbsps. (28–55g) filling into each cabbage shell.

6. Roll up each and place in the baking dish.

7. Pour 1 additional cup (237ml) marinara sauce over the shells; top with remaining parmesan and shredded mozzarella, then bake covered for 30 minutes.

8. Take off foil and bake or broil for a few extra minutes until cheese is bubbly.

CALIFORNIA ROLL IN A BOWL AND MISO SOUP

Serves 2

Cauliflower Rice

4 cups (430g–450g) cauliflower rice (about two 16-ounce bags of fresh cauliflower rice)

2 tbsps. (30ml) canned coconut milk*

1 tbsp. (15ml) rice vinegar

Pinch of salt

Toppings

1 medium cucumber, sliced into sticks

1 small carrot, sliced into sticks

½ avocado

8–10 oz. (227–283g) cooked crabmeat, chopped (or substitute same quantity sushi-grade chopped salmon or extra firm tofu)

½ tsp. (1.5g) sesame seeds for garnish (optional)

Egg, boiled for 6 minutes, peeled, and sliced in half for garnish (optional)

Sauce

3 tbsps. (45g) reduced fat mayonnaise or full-fat Greek yogurt

½ lemon, juiced

1 tsp. (5ml) soy sauce or coconut aminos

Miso Soup

1½ cups (355ml) water

½ tsp. (1.5g) dashi (optional)

1 tbsp. (17g) miso

2 ounces (60g) silken tofu, cubed

Garnishes: chopped scallions and torn seaweed

Directions

California Roll

1. Heat a nonstick skillet over medium-high heat; lightly coat with spray.

2. Add cauliflower rice to skillet. Cook for 3 to 5 minutes, stirring occasionally.

3. Add coconut aminos, vinegar, and salt and stir together. Cook for an additional 3 to 5 minutes or until most of the liquid has evaporated.

4. To assemble, divide the cauliflower rice between 2 bowls.

5. Top each bowl with half the cucumber, carrot, and crab mix.

6. Drizzle with the sauce; garnish with sesame seeds and sliced nori sheets.

Miso Soup

1. Boil water with dashi, if using.

2. Turn off the heat. Stir in the miso until well combined.

3. Add in silken tofu.

4. Garnish with chopped scallions and torn seaweed.

MEATBALLS AND DAIRY-FREE CAULI MASH

Serves 3–5

1 pound (455g) ground
lean ground beef,
turkey, chicken, or
vegan alternative

⅓ cup (32g) almond,
coconut, or oat flour

¼ cup (60ml) beef or
chicken stock

1 tsp. (5ml) avocado
or olive oil

½ yellow onion,
finely chopped

1 cup (100g) fresh
mushrooms, chopped

2 cloves garlic, chopped

1 egg

¼ cup (16g) fresh
parsley, chopped

1 tsp. (2g) dried basil

1 tsp. (2g) dried oregano

1 tsp. (5ml)
Worcestershire sauce

½ tsp. (2.8g) salt, divided

½ tsp. (1g) pepper, divided

1 large head or 2 small
heads of cauliflower

½ cup (120ml) coconut milk

½ tsp. (2g) dried thyme

½ tsp. (0.8g) garlic powder

Salt and pepper to taste
for cauli mash

Directions

Meatballs

1. Preheat the oven to 400 F (205 C). Line a large baking sheet with parchment paper and spray with oil spray.

2. Fill a large pot with water and bring to a boil. Add whole head of cauliflower or cut up florets and cook until fork tender, about 6 to 8 minutes.

3. In a large bowl, combine the flour and stock and whisk together with a fork or spatula until well combined.

4. Heat a skillet over medium heat. Add the olive oil, mushrooms, and onions and cook down for 2 to 3 minutes. Add in garlic and cook until fragrant. Season with half the salt and pepper.

5. Meanwhile add the meat, egg, Worcestershire, seasonings, herbs, and remaining salt and pepper to the flour and stock mixture.

6. Add the cooked vegetables to the meat mixture and mix well to combine.

7. To streamline the process of forming the balls, form a square with the meat mixture on a baking sheet. If you like bigger meatballs, score four lines across and three lines down, creating twelve even portions of meat; shape them into meatballs.

8. If you prefer smaller meatballs, score four rows by four columns to make 16 even sized meatballs and then shape each portion as in step 7.

9. Cook for 18 to 22 minutes or until fully cooked through. Exact cooking time will vary based on the size of your meatballs.

Cauli Mash

10. Strain the cauliflower and add to a food processor or blender with coconut milk, thyme, and garlic powder.

11. Add more coconut milk if needed to reach desired consistency.

12. Add salt and pepper to taste. Serve 2 to 3 cups (250–375g) of cauli mash along with your meatballs, garnish with parsley and lemon (optional), and enjoy.

Notes: I highly recommend doubling the recipe for meal prep.

If you are using kosher beef, it is usually pre-salted, so I'd recommend leaving salt out as an added ingredient.

You will be so happy you used the mushrooms. They really stretch your dollar because you make more meatballs for less money. When doubling the recipe, use the whole box of mushrooms.

EZ ZUCCHINI ZITI

Serves 2–3

4 zucchinis

1 package (10–14 oz./280–400g) extra firm tofu, sliced into cubes or sticks

1 cup (237ml) tomato sauce

½ cup (80g) part skim mozzarella cheese, grated

½ tsp. (0.5g) dried Italian seasoning or dried oregano

Salt to taste

Pepper to taste

1 tbsp. (6g) Parmesan cheese (optional for garnish)

¼ cup (10g) fresh basil leaves (optional for garnish)

Directions

1. Heat a skillet over medium heat with nonstick spray or oil. Add tofu to the pan and brown on each side for about 5 minutes.

2. Shave each zucchini into ribbons using a veggie peeler or spiralizer and add all to the same pan. These will cook fast and begin to wilt almost immediately. Stir for 1 to 2 minutes and remove from heat.

3. Add marinara, seasoning, salt, pepper, and any other spices of your choice.

4. Top with cheese.

BBQ LETTUCE CUPS WITH AVOCADO

Serves 2–4

Head of iceberg lettuce, romaine lettuce, or napa cabbage

Optional veggies:

- ¼ red onion, sliced
- 1 tomato, sliced
- ¼ cup (35g) pickles or other pickled vegetables

1–2 grilled or roasted chicken breasts, chopped (or cooked protein of your choice)

½ avocado, sliced

2 tbsps. (25ml) BBQ sauce (made without high fructose corn syrup)

Juice of ½ lemon

1 15-oz. (425g) can of corn or beans, drained and rinsed (optional)

¼ cup (16g) fresh cilantro or parsley, chopped (optional but encouraged)

Hot sauce or spicy mayo for garnish (optional)

It doesn't get more simple, straightforward, and nourishing than these. Stock up on these ingredients in preparation for a busy weekend—you will be so glad you did. There are so many ways to eat and enjoy them that I wanted to share two versions in the photo to give you some inspiration. If you don't want to use chicken, this works well with Perla's Perfect Salmon (see recipe on page 174) or with a vegan protein.

Directions

1. Create 3 to 4 lettuce cups as shown below.

2. Use a few layers of lettuce or cabbage to make a sturdy cup. Add in chopped chicken, tomato, onion, avocado, and beans or corn, if using.

3. Top with lemon juice and BBQ sauce. Garnish with pickles, cilantro or parsley, and some extra spicy sauce if you like.

AHI SHAWARMA WRAPS

Serves 2–3

2 tsps. (10ml) olive, avocado, or coconut oil

1½ cups (150g) chopped mushrooms

¼ white onion, chopped

2 cloves garlic, crushed or finely minced

12 oz. (340g) ahi tuna, chopped (or can also use shrimp, white fish, firm tofu, or raw chicken breast)

2 tsps. (10g) shawarma seasoning (I like the one by Pereg Natural)

Pinch of salt

2–4 high fiber tortillas (ideally with at least 3 grams fiber per serving)

2 tbsps. (15g) roasted red bell peppers, chopped (can be bought already roasted in a jar)

Head romaine or iceberg lettuce, chopped

¼ fresh red onion, diced

2 tbsps. (8g) fresh parsley, chopped

2 tbsps. (30g) tahini

½ lemon, juiced

2 tbsps. (30ml) water

Directions

1. Spray a pan with oil spray; sauté 1½ cups (150g) chopped mushrooms, ¼ onion, and 2 cloves of chopped garlic over low to medium heat for 2 to 3 minutes.

2. In a small bowl, mix tahini with lemon and water until smooth and well combined; set aside.

3. Add chopped ahi tuna (you can buy it frozen and thaw it in the fridge).

4. Add a very generous amount of shawarma seasoning. It should coat the ahi and vegetables. Add a small sprinkle of salt.

5. Lay out high fiber tortillas and top each evenly with the chopped roasted red peppers, a handful of shredded lettuce, and the shawarma ahi mix, along with fresh onion and parsley. Drizzle with tahini sauce and enjoy.

Note: if you can't find shawarma seasoning, mix together:

2 tbsps. (13g) sweet paprika
1 tbsp. (6g) allspice
1 tbsp. (9g) cumin
2 tsps. (6g) turmeric
1 tsp. (3g) cinnamon
1 tsp. (1.6g) garlic powder
1 tsp. (2.4g) onion powder
½ tsp. (1.6g) ground ginger
½ tsp. (0.8g) chili flakes (optional)

VEGGIE FRIED "RICE" AND SEASONED TOFU STEAK

Serves 2–3

Fried Rice

1–2 garlic cloves, crushed or minced

16 oz. (1 lb./455g) of either cauliflower rice (frozen or fresh) or hearts of palm rice (canned, rinsed and drained well)

3 carrots, shredded, or 2 cups (240g) pre-grated carrots

1 egg

2 tsp. (10ml) low sodium soy sauce or coconut aminos

1 tsp. (5ml) toasted sesame oil

¼ tsp. (1.4g) salt

Pepper to taste

2 green onions, chopped

1 tsp. (1.5g) sesame seeds for garnish

Tofu Steak

1 box firm tofu (10–14 oz./280–400g), drained and pressed to help remove excess liquid

3 tbsp. (32g) nutritional yeast

1 tsp. (1.6g) garlic powder

1 tsp. (2.4g) onion powder

½ tsp. (0.5g) oregano

½ tsp. (2g) chili powder

½ tsp. (1g) paprika

¼ tsp. (0.6g) pepper

Directions

Fried Rice

1. Heat a skillet over medium heat; spray with oil spray.

2. Add garlic, veggie rice, 1 chopped green onion, shredded carrots, salt, and pepper to skillet and mix. Stir fry over medium heat for 3 to 5 minutes until cauliflower, carrots, and green onion have wilted and become fragrant.

3. Make a well in the center of the skillet and add the cracked egg. After about a minute, scramble the egg using a spatula, working it into the cauliflower and other vegetables in the pan. Turn off the heat.

4. Drizzle soy sauce and sesame oil over the skillet and mix again.

5. Top with remaining green onion and sesame seeds.

Tofu Steak

6. Wrap firm tofu with a paper towel and place under a heavy pan to remove excess liquid; leave it under pressure for at least 30 minutes and up to 2 hours. Slice tofu lengthwise into "steaks."

Love the Food that Loves You Back

7. To a large plate or dish, add the nutritional yeast and remaining spices and seasonings. Use a fork or spoon to mix together. One at a time, place each steak onto the plate and coat each side with the seasoning rub.

8. Heat a skillet or grill pan over medium heat and add oil spray. Cook the tofu for 2 to 3 minutes on each side. Serve the tofu steaks along with the cauliflower fried rice and enjoy.

EASY ROASTED CHICKEN AND EGGPLANT PARMIGIANA "NOODLES"

Serves 4

1 whole chicken (about 3 pounds/1,360g)

1 tbsp. (2.4g) onion powder

Salt and pepper

3 tbsps. (45ml) olive oil

1 lemon

2 large eggplants, peeled and cut into long straw or French fry-like shapes (to a thickness of ¼ inch/~0.6cm)

⅓ cup (40g) breadcrumbs made of whole wheat or other high fiber grain

1 tsp. (5.7g) salt

1 tsp. (1.6g) garlic powder

1 tsp. (2g) oregano

1 cup (237ml) marinara sauce

¼ cup (25g) Parmesan cheese (traditional or dairy free), grated

Notes: To make this vegan, pair with roasted tofu, tempeh, edamame, or lupini beans instead of chicken.

For a shortcut, pair with a rotisserie chicken rather than roasting your own.

Directions

1. Preheat oven to 350 F (175 C).

2. In a roasting pan or cooking dish, add whole chicken and drizzle with olive oil. Season generously with salt, pepper, and onion powder. Squeeze half the lemon into the chicken cavity, then squeeze the remaining lemon over the chicken. Cook for one hour and 20 minutes or until a meat thermometer inserted into the thickest part of the thigh reads 165 degrees F (74 degrees C).

3. While the chicken is cooking, spray oil in large pan over medium heat and place cut up eggplant pieces in the pan. Cook down for about 5 minutes.

4. To a flat pan or a regular sized pan, add breadcrumbs, salt, garlic powder, and oregano; toast until fragrant.

5. Add marinara sauce to eggplant noodles and stir for 2 minutes. Remove from pan and add to a bowl. Set aside.

6. Add breadcrumbs and parmesan cheese to the eggplant noodles in the bowl.

7. Remove chicken from oven and let cool.

8. Enjoy the eggplant parmigiana noodles with a piece of roasted chicken. Top with parsley to garnish.

CHICKEN CHOMP

Serves 6–8

8 pieces cut up chicken plus 2 chicken breasts with bone in (optional to remove skin)

2 cups (340g) uncooked quinoa

4 cups (946ml) of water, or 2 cups (473ml) of water and 2 cups (473ml) of low sodium broth

¾ cup (177ml) BBQ sauce (made without high fructose corn syrup)

½ cup (60g) seasoned breadcrumbs

2 onions, sliced

3–4 carrots, diced

3–4 celery stalks, diced

My amazing daughter Olivia named this recipe. It's her absolute favorite, and I'm confident you will watch your kids impress you as they chomp it down with delight.

Directions

1. Preheat the oven to 400 F (205 C). Pour quinoa and water into a 9-x-13-inch (23-cm-x-33-cm) or larger baking dish. Add onions and carrots to the pan and stir together, then set pan aside.

2. In a separate bowl, toss BBQ sauce with chicken until all of the chicken is coated. Top the quinoa and veggies with the BBQ-coated chicken.

3. Place breadcrumbs on a plate and sprinkle each piece of chicken with a thin layer of breadcrumbs. (Optional to coat the top side of the chicken only.)

4. Cover with tin foil and bake for an hour and fifteen minutes.

5. Bake uncovered for an additional 15 minutes or until the chicken is fully cooked. Serve with craveable veggies and enjoy.

CAULIFLOWER NACHOS

Serves 1-2

3-4 cups (300–400g) cauliflower florets, washed, cleaned, and cut into bite-size pieces one to two inches (2.5–5 cm) long

Olive oil spray or 2 tsp. (10ml) olive or coconut oil

1 tsp. (3g) cumin

¼ tsp. (1g) turmeric

1 tsp. (3g) Tajín or chili lime seasoning

4-6 oz. (113–170g) lean ground meat, turkey, or meatless crumbles, cooked

3 tbsps. (42g) cheese, shredded: choose from part skim cheddar, mozzarella, or Mexican cheese blend

¼ cup (70g) plain unsweetened Greek yogurt

2 tbsps. (25g) tomatoes, chopped

½ lime, sliced into two equal wedges for garnish

1 tbsp. (3g) fresh cilantro, chopped (optional)

¼ cup (13g) red onions, sliced (optional)

If you're still new to veggies, you will discover that cauliflower nachos always dazzle the newbies. This is one of the most popular recipes for people just getting started with their health journey. One bite and you'll realize that healthy eating can be enjoyable and delicious.

Directions

1. Preheat the oven to 400 F (205 C).

2. Line a baking sheet with parchment paper and set aside.

3. In a large mixing bowl, add cauliflower; spray cauliflower with oil spray (or add oil).

4. Toss to evenly coat the cauliflower.

5. Add seasonings and toss again.

6. Place seasoned cauliflower on a single layer on the baking sheet and bake for 30 minutes.

7. While the cauliflower is roasting, brown and cook the meat (or vegetarian crumbles) in a nonstick skillet.

8. Safely remove the cauliflower from the oven and top evenly with meat and cheese. Return the cauliflower to the oven and cook an additional 2 to 5 minutes or until the cheese is bubbly. (You can optionally change the oven setting to low broil and cook for 2 to 3 minutes extra so the cheese and cauliflower crisp up at the edges).

9. Carefully remove the cauliflower nachos from the sheet pan and transfer to a serving dish. Top with Greek yogurt, tomatoes, lime wedges, and cilantro and onions (if using).

Note: Optional to either cook the meat or meatless grounds with the onions or reserve the raw onions as a garnish on top of the nachos.

LOW CARB SUSHI BURRITO

Serves 2

Parchment paper

Plastic wrap (optional)

4 oz. (113g) cooked crabmeat (or cooked shrimp), cleaned and chopped

4 oz. (113g) sushi-grade raw tuna, salmon, or extra firm tofu, chopped

2 tsps. (10ml) low sodium soy sauce or coconut aminos

1 tsp. (5ml) sesame oil

1 tsp. (5g) mayonnaise

½ avocado, sliced

½ English cucumber or 1–2 Persian cucumbers, sliced

1 head iceberg lettuce, with core removed and larger leaves intact

½ tsp. (3g) prepared wasabi (optional)

1 tbsp. (15ml) miso dressing, sesame ginger dressing, lemon juice, or spicy mayo (optional)

Directions

1. Chop the crabmeat and mix with miso or ginger dressing, lemon juice, or spicy mayo.

2. In a separate bowl, add tuna, salmon, or tofu, then add sesame oil, soy sauce or coconut aminos, and optional wasabi.

3. On a clean surface, lay a large sheet of parchment paper. Place 2 to 3 layers of large iceberg lettuce leaves on top to make 2 lettuce wraps. Fill each lettuce wrap with half the chopped crabmeat, tuna, cucumber, and avocado.

4. Wrap like a burrito using parchment paper. Optionally, burritos can be fastened more tightly with a layer of plastic wrap.

5. Slice in half and repeat with remaining ingredients. Serve with pickled ginger, soy sauce (optional) wasabi, and spicy mayonnaise.

BEEF AND SHIRATAKI NOODLES

Serves 3-4

1–1¼ lb. (454–567g) lean steak, sliced into thin strips

2 eggs

4 8-ounce bags (225g) shirataki noodles, drained

½ cup (55g) shredded carrots

2 cups (220g) sugar snap peas, broccoli florets, or snow peas

Additional cup (100g) of bean sprouts and/ or sliced mushrooms (optional)

1 tsp. (2.4g) onion powder

Pinch salt and pepper (optional)

¼ cup (60ml) ketchup (made without high fructose corn syrup)

3 tbsps. (45ml) peanut butter powder

2 tbsps. (30ml) low sodium soy sauce

2 tbsps. (30ml) rice vinegar

5 cloves garlic, chopped

1 tbsp. (10g) cornstarch

2 tbsps. (30ml) water

2 limes, quartered for garnish

2 tbsps. (15g) peanuts for garnish, crushed

2 tbsps. (6g) scallions, chopped

Red chili flakes for garnish (optional)

This pad Thai inspired recipe makes an incredible dinner. Don't skip the lime. It adds a nice pop to the meal.

Directions

1. Make the sauce in a small bowl by mixing together the peanut butter powder, ketchup, rice vinegar, and soy sauce. Set aside.

2. Season the beef with onion powder, salt, and pepper.

3. Sauté the beef in a large skillet for 1 to 2 minutes, using either a nonstick pan or a pan sprayed with coconut, olive, or avocado oil.

4. Add chopped garlic and cook for an additional minute.

5. Add carrots, snap peas, noodles, and sauce to the beef and cook for an additional 2 to 3 minutes or until meat is cooked through. Stir and mix well.

6. In a small bowl, mix 1 tbsp. (10g) of cornstarch with 2 tbsps. (30ml) of water, then pour the cornstarch mix into the pan along with the meat and veggies. This will help thicken the sauce because the shirataki noodles and veggies will have released a lot of excess water. Cook for an additional minute or two, stirring often.

7. Divide onto plates and garnish with scallions and peanuts. Serve with a large wedge of lime and optional chili flakes.

MISO MAPLE CHICKEN THIGHS AND MELTED CABBAGE

Serves 4–5

2 lbs. (900g) chicken thighs, skinless, either boneless or bone in

2 tbsps. (34g) white miso paste

4 tbsps. (60ml) pure maple syrup

3 heads of garlic, minced

1 tbsp. (6g) fresh ginger, grated

1 tbsp. (15ml) sesame oil

1 tbsp. (15ml) rice wine vinegar

Juice of 1 large orange

8–10 cups (700–900g) cabbage or kale, shredded

2 shallots, sliced

Directions

1. Preheat the oven to 400 F (205 C).

2. In a mixing bowl, combine the sauce ingredients: miso paste, maple syrup, garlic, ginger, oil, vinegar, and juice. Set aside.

3. Spray a large baking dish with oil spray.

4. Lay shredded cabbage or kale evenly across the baking sheet.

5. Top veggies with the chicken thighs.

6. Pour sauce over the whole dish and top with chopped shallots.

7. Cover tightly with foil and bake.

8. Bake for 25 minutes if using boneless chicken thighs and 50 to 65 minutes if using bone-in chicken thighs.

Note: Use a meat thermometer to ensure chicken is cooked to an internal temperature of 165 F (74 C) if concerned about a larger piece being cooked through.

POWER PROTEINS

CLOUD BREAD

If you are new to me and my content, you may not know what my cloud breads are, but when I was pregnant with my baby number 3, cloud bread was all I craved! And it quickly became one of the first videos in my viral video series I created to grow my TikTok following in 2020. Almost every day I experimented with a new fun way to enjoy the cloud bread recipe, most of the time inspired by a suggestion from someone in my comments. If it weren't for my amazing community, some of the best of these recipes, like the burrito or cinnamon rolls, wouldn't even exist, and I am so so grateful for their help!

STANDARD CLOUD BREAD

Serves 1

Regular Cloud Bread

¾ cup (177ml) fresh liquid
   egg whites (4 egg whites)

2½ tsp. (7g) cornstarch,
   almond flour, or
   arrowroot starch

Supersized Cloud Bread

1 cup (237ml) of fresh
   liquid egg whites
   (5–6 eggs)

1 tbsp. (8g) cornstarch,
   almond flour, or
   arrowroot starch or flour

Directions

1. Preheat oven to 300 F (150 C).

2. Beat egg whites until stiff peaks form, about 2 to 3 minutes.

3. Add in cornstarch, almond flour, or arrowroot starch or flour.

4. Beat again until mixed.

5. Spread evenly on a greased baking sheet, 9-x-13 inch (23-x-33 cm) or similar.

6. Bake for 23 to 25 minutes.

> **Note:** If using almond flour, the cloud bread will be a bit denser and flatter.

CLOUD BREAD BURRITO

Serves 1

¾ cup (177ml) egg whites

2½ tsp. (8g) cornstarch

2–4 tbsp. (30–65g) refried beans or smashed black beans

¼ avocado, sliced

1 tbsp. (8g) cheese or dairy-free cheese alternative, shredded

1 tbsp. (15ml) salsa

Directions

1. Preheat oven to 300 F (150 C).

2. Beat egg whites, then beat in cornstarch.

3. Spread on baking sheet and bake for 23 minutes at 300 F (150 C).

4. Let cool; add beans, avocado, cheese, and salsa.

5. Roll it up and enjoy with additional veggies for dinner.

CLOUD BREAD CINNAMON ROLLS

Serves 1

Cloud Bread

1 cup (237ml) egg whites

1 tbsp. (8g) cornstarch, arrowroot, almond flour, or tapioca flour

Filling

1 tbsp. (14g) whipped butter or vegan butter

1 tbsp. (14g) brown sugar or alternative sweetener equivalent (such as dark agave syrup)

1 tsp. (3g) cinnamon

1 tsp. (3g) pecans, chopped (optional)

Icing

¼ cup (60g) plain yogurt (can be Greek or dairy free)

1 to 3 tbsps. (15–45ml) almond milk, depending on desired consistency

2 tbsps. (25g) sugar or sugar replacement (I like a monk fruit or stevia blend)

½ tsp. (2.5ml) vanilla extract

Directions

1. Preheat oven to 300 F (150 C).

2. Line a baking sheet with parchment paper and spray well with nonstick spray; set aside.

3. In a large glass bowl, use an electric mixer to beat egg whites; when egg whites are fluffy and no liquid remains, add cornstarch and beat again.

4. Spread cloud bread on a baking sheet; bake at 300 F (150 C) for 23 minutes.

5. Make filling by heating up butter until it liquefies. (I heat my butter in the microwave for about 20 seconds.) Stir in brown sugar and cinnamon and set aside.

6. Make icing by mixing all of the icing ingredients together. Set aside.

7. Assembly: When cloud bread is finished baking and has cooled, spread with filling and roll tightly. Slice and serve with icing.

CLOUD BREAD PIZZA

Serves 1

4 egg whites

2½ tsp. (8g) cornstarch

2 tbsps. (30ml) tomato sauce for pizza topping

3 tbsps. (42g) reduced fat cheese, shredded, for pizza topping

Vegetables prepared to top pizza (optional)— your choice:

- Mushrooms, sliced
- Kale, chopped
- Bell peppers, chopped
- Broccoli florets, chopped small
- Yellow onion, chopped
- Black olives, sliced
- Basil leaves, fresh

Directions

1. Bake cloud bread according to steps 1–4 on previous page.

2. Remove from oven and top with tomato sauce, cheese, and toppings of your choice.

3. Increase temperature to 400 F (205 C), or to a low broil.

4. Place pizza back in the oven and cook until the cheese is bubbly, approximately 2 to 5 minutes, checking frequently to make sure pizza does not burn.

AVOCADO TOAST

Serves 1

4 egg whites (¾ cup/177ml)

2½ tsp. (8g) cornstarch

¼ large avocado or ½ small one, either sliced thinly or smashed with lemon juice

¼ cup (45g) sliced cherry tomatoes or heirloom tomatoes

2 tbsps. (25g) pickled red onion (see section on sauces and dips)

Flaky sea salt and cracked black pepper

Pinch of red chili flakes (optional)

Directions

1. Bake the cloud bread as in previous directions.

2. Once it's cool enough to touch, add avocado and layer with additional ingredients.

3. Enjoy!

CLOUD BREAD CINNAMON PANCAKES

Serves 1

1 cup (237ml) egg whites

1 tbsp. (8g) cornstarch, almond flour, or arrowroot starch

2 tbsps. (25g) monk fruit sugar substitute or 2 packets of stevia

½ tbsp. (4.5g) cinnamon

⅓ tsp. (2g) salt

¼ tsp. (1.5ml) vanilla extract

1 tsp. (5g) butter, ghee, or coconut oil

½ tsp. (1.3g) powdered sugar

Directions

1. Beat 1 cup (237ml) egg whites until big and cloud-like.

2. Add in 1 tbsp. (8g) cornstarch, almond flour, or arrowroot.

3. Add in 1 tbsp. (12.5g) monk fruit sweetener or one packet stevia, cinnamon, salt, and vanilla extract to the raw egg white batter. Beat again.

4. Grease a skillet with butter or oil and bring to medium heat. Spoon ⅓ cup (80ml) cloud bread "pancake batter" into the pan in the same way as you would cook pancakes. After 2 to 3 minutes, flip and cook for an additional 2 to 3 minutes on the other side.

5. Top with cinnamon or optional powdered sugar (or another sweetener) and enjoy.

Note: Pairs well with fruit as a complete breakfast.

PB&J CLOUD BREAD

Serves 1

1 cup (237ml) liquid
egg whites

1 tbsp. (8g) cornstarch,
almond flour,
or arrowroot

1 cup (150g) frozen berries,
choose blackberries,
raspberries, or a mixed
blend; if you want to
use fresh, add 1–2 tbsps.
(15–30ml) of water to
prevent burning

2 tsp. (8g) monk fruit
sweetener or 1 tsp.
(7g) honey

1 tbsp. (11g) chia seeds

2 tbsps. (30g) peanut
butter powder

1½ tbsps. (23ml) water

½ tsp. (2.5ml)
vanilla extract

Pinch of cinnamon

Directions

1. Prepare cloud bread according to previous instructions using 1 cup (237ml) egg whites. While the cloud bread bakes, prepare the jam by heating a saucepan up to medium heat and adding the frozen berries. Stir continuously to melt and mash together. Stir in chia seeds and sweetener. Remove from the saucepan and transfer to a heatproof bowl. Let cool and thicken in the fridge.

2. Prepare the peanut spread by mixing the peanut butter powder with water, vanilla, and cinnamon. (Note that hot water blends a bit better. Add a pinch of salt if you like.)

3. When the cloud bread is fully cooked and cool enough to handle, slice in half. Spread "peanut butter" and "jelly" on the cloud bread halves and eat halves together as a sandwich.

EVERYTHING BUT THE BAGEL CLOUD BREAD

Serves 1

1 cup (237ml) liquid
  egg whites

1 tbsp. (8g) cornstarch,
  arrowroot or almond flour

1 tbsp. (15g) light
  cream cheese

1 tbsp. (3g)
  chives, chopped

1 tsp. (3g) "everything"
  bagel seasoning

1½ oz. (44g) lox (optional)

1 tsp. (3g) capers, lemon
  slices, and slices of red
  onion (optional)

Directions

1. Preheat the oven to 300 F (150 C).

2. Beat egg whites with an electric mixer for about 2 to 3 minutes until stiff peaks form. (I use egg whites from a carton of liquid egg whites, but you can also separate fresh egg whites to get to a cup.)

3. Add in 1 tbsp. (8g) cornstarch, almond flour, or arrowroot starch or flour.

4. Beat again until mixed.

5. Spread evenly on a greased baking sheet.

6. Bake for 23 to 25 minutes.

7. When cool, add light cream cheese, chives, and everything bagel seasoning.

8. For a flavor and protein boost, you can add smoked salmon and capers.

WONDER WHIPS

Cloud breads were to my third pregnancy as wonder whips were to my second pregnancy! I guess my boys were really craving lots of lean protein. I remember how almost every day at around eleven in the morning I would feel like a bottomless pit. There were times I found myself eating three servings of these wonder whips at a time just to make me feel calm and satisfied. Trust me, if you're hungry for sweets, they work. They're so easy to make, satisfying to your sweet tooth, and keep you feeling full for a while. If you're dairy free, it would make sense to make these recipes with silken tofu substituted for the yogurt ingredient because it's equally high in protein. Using a dairy-free yogurt might work to satisfy your sweet tooth but won't give you as much of the protein you may need to satisfy your hunger. You can try stirring in a vegan protein powder to help make up the difference.

Fun Twist! You can also turn any of these recipes into a frozen yogurt bark!

OG PEANUT BUTTER WONDER WHIP

Serves 1

¾ cup (177ml) plain
  unsweetened
  Greek yogurt

2 tbsps. (30g) peanut
  butter powder

2 tbsps. (30ml)
  unsweetened almond
  milk, light coffee creamer,
  or milk of your choice

Stevia to taste (~2 packets
  or 1½ droppers of
  liquid stevia)

1 tbsp. (9g) crushed
  peanuts or cocoa nibs
  (optional)

Directions

1. Mix all ingredients together in a bowl using a
   fork, spoon, or whisk and enjoy.

2. To turn into a frozen bark: Line a baking sheet
   or ceramic plate with parchment paper. Mix
   the recipe's ingredients together, then evenly
   spread the yogurt mixture on the tray until it's
   about 1 inch thick. Freeze for 2 hours or longer
   and enjoy.

LEMON BLUEBERRY WONDER WHIP

Serves 1

¾ cup (177ml) Greek yogurt (nonfat or 2 percent)

¼ lemon, juiced

½ tsp. (2g) fresh zest of lemon

½ tsp. (2g) stevia or monk fruit

2 tbsps. unsweetened milk of your choice, like almond, coconut, or oat milk

½ cup (80g) fresh or frozen blueberries

1 tbsp. (6g) slivered almonds (optional)

Directions

1. Mix all ingredients together in a bowl using a fork, spoon, or whisk.

2. Top with slivered almonds if using, and enjoy!

Note: If you are using frozen blueberries, you can build the bowl backward by adding the frozen blueberries first (½ cup/70g); add berries to the first line of the Craving Crusher bowl if using. Microwave covered for 40 seconds in a microwave-safe bowl until it makes a melted sauce. Add the remaining ingredients. Stir together well and enjoy.

To turn into a frozen bark, line a baking sheet or ceramic plate with parchment paper. Mix the ingredients of the recipe together, then evenly spread the yogurt mixture on the tray until it's about 1 inch thick. Freeze for 2 hours or longer and enjoy.

BIRTHDAY "CAKE" WONDER WHIP

Serves 1

½ cup (140g) plain unsweetened Greek yogurt

2 tbsps. (30) milk of your choice

¼ tsp. (1.5ml) vanilla & butter extract

2–3 packets stevia or sweetener of your choice

1 tsp. (2g) all-natural sprinkles or 1½ tbsp. (23g) crushed freeze-dried raspberries and blueberries

Directions

1. Place all ingredients in a bowl.

2. Whip together well with a fork, spoon, or whisk.

3. Add the sprinkles on top and enjoy!

FRUITY WEBBLE WONDER WHIP

Serves 1

1 cup (280g) nonfat Greek yogurt

2 tbsps. (30ml) blueberry lavender almond milk, like the kind from Trader Joe's (or substitute unsweetened vanilla almond milk)

½ tsp. (5ml) coconut extract

1–2 packets stevia

¼ cup (35g) freeze-dried strawberries

¼ cup (35g) freeze-dried blueberries

In addition to being higher in protein and lower in artificial ingredients, the fruity webble wonder whip has half the sugar content compared to 1 cup sugary cereal prepared with milk.

Directions

1. Add everything but the freeze-dried fruit to a bowl and whip with a fork, whisk, or spoon.

2. Top with fruit and enjoy.

Tips: You can use fresh fruit as well. Freeze-dried fruit is a little crispier, which adds a nice crunch.

FROWHOAS

FroWhoas were yet another viral recipe series of mine because it honestly takes a protein shake to a whole new level. I call them *FroWhoas* because although they almost taste like a better version of frozen yogurt, there's no yogurt in them. Plus, when you see the giant serving size and taste it, you just might scream "*Whoa!*"

STANDARD FROWHOA

Serves 1

1 cup (150g) ice

1 cup (237ml) unsweetened almond milk or water

Stevia sweetener to taste (optional)

¼–½ tsp. (0.6–1.25g) xanthan gum (optional)

1 scoop (2 tbsps./30g) protein powder. I use whey or plant-based Shakeology® or BODi® Recover.

Note: Xanthan gum is a soluble fiber commonly used to thicken or stabilize foods. As with all fibers, in large quantities, this gum can have a laxative effect. Use caution if you have IBS or a sensitive stomach, and omit if needed.

Directions

1. Blend all of the ingredients together for at least 60 to 90 seconds.

CHOCZINI FROWHOA

Serves 1

1 cup (237ml)
  unsweetened
  almond milk

1 scoop (2 tbsps./30g)
  protein powder; I
  use whey or plant-
  based Shakeology® or
  BODi® Recover

1 cup (150g) frozen raw
  zucchini, chopped (if
  using fresh zucchini,
  keep in mind it's easier to
  chop before freezing)

All summer long, I am stocking up on zucchinis, slicing them and freezing them. When you freeze raw slices of zucchini and put them into a shake (in place of ice), it makes your smoothie so thick and creamy but doesn't change the taste! It is like magic, just trust me on this one.

Directions

1. Blend all ingredients together and enjoy!

CHOCZINI ICE CREAM

Serves 1

¾ cup (177ml)
unsweetened
almond milk

1 cup (150g) frozen
raw zucchini, washed
and sliced

1 scoop (2 tbsps./30g)
chocolate protein
powder; I use whey
protein or plant-
based Shakeology® or
BODi® recover

½ banana

1 tbsp. (7.5g) cacao nibs

To make it sweeter, you
can optionally add 1 tsp.
(2.5g) of stevia, monk
fruit, or coconut sugar

Directions

1. Blend all ingredients together and enjoy!

Note: Add dark chocolate shavings on top for
optional garnish.

SNICKERS FROWHOA

Serves 1

¾ cup (177ml) unsweetened milk of your choice

1 cup (150g) frozen raw zucchini

½ scoop (1 tbsp./15g) chocolate protein powder; I use either whey protein or plant-based Shakeology® or BODi® Recover

2 tbsps. (30g) peanut butter powder

⅛ tsp. (0.3g) xanthan gum (totally optional)

½ tsp. (2.5ml) butter extract and caramel extract

½ tbsp. (4g) crushed peanuts (optional)

½ tbsp. (11g) date syrup for garnish (optional)

Directions

1. Blend all ingredients together and enjoy!!

MEAT, CHICKEN & FISH

GO-TO TUNA

Serves 1–2

- 1 can (5 oz./142g) albacore tuna, packed in water and drained
- 1 tbsp. (15g) avocado mayonnaise or reduced fat mayonnaise
- 1 tbsp. (17.5g) Greek yogurt
- ¼ tsp. (1.4g) salt
- ¼ tsp. (0.4g) garlic powder
- ½ tsp. (3g) Dijon mustard

Tuna is a staple in my house and one of my kid's favorite proteins. I typically make four to five servings at a time because it lasts up to three days in the fridge and we all love it.

Directions

1. Wear clean rubber gloves or use very clean hands to mix together all of the ingredients in a bowl.

2. Alternatively, you can use the back of a fork to mash thoroughly until very well combined.

Crunchy variation: Add 2 tbsps. (15g) chopped celery

Make it heartier: Add in a chopped hard-boiled egg

Make it more Mediterranean: Add 1 tbsp. (4g) fresh chopped parsley and dill and the juice of half a lemon.

Bell pepper tuna melt variation: Prepare the recipe according to the directions above. Divide between two large bell pepper halves. Top with 2 tbsps. (30g) shredded cheese and broil for 2 to 3 minutes until the cheese is golden brown and bubbly. Add scallions and chili flakes for garnish (optional).

SILVER EGG SALAD

Serves 2–4

6 hard-boiled eggs, boiled for 7 minutes, with two to three yolks removed and reserved (you can use them in another recipe to emulsify a vinaigrette)

2 tbsps. (30ml) high-quality extra-virgin olive oil

¼ cup (25g) chopped scallions

¼-½ tsp. (1.4–2.8g) sea salt

Fresh cracked pepper

Red chili flakes to taste (optional)

My husband's good friend growing up, Ira Silver, was South African, and this is how his family prepared egg salad. It was a huge change from the heavy mayonnaise-based egg salads I grew up eating as a kid, and once I tried this version, I was instantly hooked.

Directions

1. Cut each egg into about 6 pieces.

2. Mix all of the ingredients together well, leaving large chunks of egg. Layer over toasted whole grain bread with a thick slice of a good tomato and sprinkled chives on top for a delicious breakfast, lunch, or snack.

MEAT LOVERS MEAT

Serves 10–12

3–4 pounds (1,360–1,820g) French roast (boneless chuck or rolled rump roast)

1 16-oz. (473ml) bottle of your favorite BBQ sauce, garlic sauce, teriyaki sauce, or stir fry sauce

2 large yellow onions, sliced

1 large cabbage or 4–6 carrots, sliced or shredded (optional)

Warning: If you make this recipe for a crowd, it will be the only recipe they will talk about. It is literally everyone's favorite, which is great for you because it is super easy to make.

Directions

1. Preheat the oven to 350 F (175 C).

2. In a 9-x-13-inch (23-x-33-cm) baking dish, spread cabbage and onions evenly on the bottom.

3. Top with roast and cover evenly with sauce.

4. Seal tightly with foil and cook for 4 hours.

YEAR-ROUND INSTANT POT TURKEY BREAST

Serves 4–6

Nonstick cooking spray

Half a raw, bone-in turkey breast

1 (10-oz./284g) package mirepoix (mixed onion, celery, and carrots), or chop your own using 1–2 onions, 3 celery stalks, and 2–3 large carrots

1 green bell pepper, thickly sliced

¼ cup (60ml) sweet chili sauce (corn syrup-free), or apricot jam

¼ cup (60ml) water

2 medium apples or pears, chopped (optional)

2 tbsps. (7g) chopped fresh sage leaves (or 2 tsp. [2g] dried sage, or 1 tsp. [1g] ground sage)

1–2 tbsps. (15–30ml) coconut aminos or reduced sodium soy sauce (adds a really yummy salty/ savory element)

Additional garlic powder, dried thyme, onion powder, and black pepper (optional).

This recipe is great if you are on a budget because turkey breast is usually one of the better priced items in the fresh poultry aisle and makes for an excellent lean protein source. We usually eat it hot right out of the pressure cooker, but it's also great as leftovers to use in salads, wraps, and sandwiches. To make this a complete dinner, double the quantity of vegetables by adding in 2 to 3 turnips, rutabagas, or celery roots to the bottom of the pot.

Directions

1. Coat pressure cooker with nonstick spray.

2. Add chopped vegetables to pressure cooker and top with turkey breast, followed by the seasoning, chili sauce or jam, water, apples or pears (if using), and soy sauce; stir to combine.

3. Seal lid. Set Instant Pot to "Poultry" or "High Pressure" for 25 minutes. If it is a larger turkey breast, make sure to cook it for a bit longer to make sure it is fully cooked.

4. Once cycle is complete, release pressure immediately, being sure to keep clear of steam.

5. Remove turkey breast to a carving board. Slice; remove bone. Set aside.

6. Serve with cooked veggies and enjoy.

PERLA'S PERFECT SALMON

Serves 3-4

1 lb. (454g) salmon

1½ tsp. (8ml) olive oil

½ tsp. (0.8g) garlic powder

½ tsp. (2.8g) salt

1 tsp. (1g) dry dill

Lemon slices for serving

If you've been following me on Instagram stories for at least a few months, there's no way you haven't seen me eating or preparing this salmon. 90 percent of the time I think about making a new salmon recipe, I end up saying, "Nah—I'm sticking to what I know works." You can't go wrong with this. Kids like it, friends like it, and it tastes great for the next couple days cold or at room temp. It's a classic recipe you'll want to make on repeat and serve with any salad, grain, or side.

Directions

1. Preheat the oven to 400 F (205 C).

2. Line a baking sheet with parchment paper. Place salmon on the baking sheet skin side down.

3. Rub the flesh of the salmon with the olive oil.

4. Sprinkle an even layer of garlic powder, salt, and dill over the salmon.

5. Bake for 17 to 19 minutes.

6. If using an air fryer, cook at 400 F (205 C) for 7 to 10 minutes.

7. It is great served warm, cold, or at room temperature.

EASY PROTEIN NUGGETS WITH YOGURT DILL SAUCE

Serves 2–3

10 oz. (284g) canned tuna, chicken, or crumbled extra firm tofu, with all excess liquid removed

1 egg or 3 tbsps. (45ml) liquid egg substitute

½ cup (80g) part skim mozzarella cheese or vegan alternative, shredded

⅛ tsp. (0.2g) garlic powder or 1 clove of garlic, minced

2 tbsps. (15g) whole wheat or panko breadcrumbs (optional)

¼ cup (70g) plain Greek yogurt

1 tsp. (15g) dry dill or 1 tbsp. (3.5g) fresh dill, chopped

Juice of ½ lemon, about 1½ tbsps. (22ml) lemon juice

Pinch of salt and pepper

Directions

Protein Nuggets

1. Preheat the oven or air fryer to 375 F (190 C). If using an oven, line a baking sheet with parchment paper and set aside.

2. Add protein, egg, cheese, and garlic to a bowl or food processor and mix well until combined.

3. Form into rounded rectangles or discs. Sprinkle a light layer of breadcrumbs on top to add a bit of texture (optional).

4. Place nuggets on the lined baking sheet and bake for 20 to 25 minutes in the oven; if using an air fryer, cook nuggets in the air fryer basket for 10 to 12 minutes. Nuggets should be golden brown and crispy on the outside.

Yogurt Dill Sauce

5. Whisk together the yogurt, dill, lemon, salt, and pepper.

Note: Serve with shredded cabbage or coleslaw mix and use the yogurt dill sauce as your dressing.

SALMON CAKES

Serves 3–4

1 can (14.75-ounce/420g)
  salmon, drained with
  bones removed

2 green onions,
  thinly sliced

1 tbsp. (3.5g) fresh
  dill, chopped

½ cup (60g) whole
  wheat breadcrumbs
  (or gluten free whole
  grain breadcrumbs)

¼ cup (70g) Greek
  yogurt (either 2 percent
  or full fat)

1 tbsp. (15ml) lemon juice

1 tbsp. (15g) Dijon mustard

1 large egg, beaten

½ tsp. (1g) black pepper

Cooking spray

This recipe is a spin on the protein nuggets with a few more fresh ingredients to make the salmon pop. It can easily be made with fresh cooked salmon or with canned tuna if you don't have canned salmon.

Directions

1. Add all ingredients (except for cooking spray) into a large bowl and mix until well incorporated.

2. Using your hands, form into 8 small patties. Chill patties until ready to cook.

3. Spray cooking spray over a large pan; preheat pan over medium-high heat.

4. Cook patties until golden and crispy, about 2 to 3 minutes per side.

5. Serve salmon patties with leafy greens and lemon wedges if desired.

6. These would also be great in a wrap served with some roasted vegetables and avocado.

SUPERSIZED BURGERS

Serves 3–4

16 oz. (454g) raw cauliflower rice (either bought prepared or made at home using a box grater or food processor to shred a head of cauliflower into rice-like pieces)

1 lb. (454g) raw ground beef

½ tsp. (2.8g) salt

¼ tsp. (0.6g) black pepper

¼ tsp. (0.75g) cumin

¼ tsp. (0.4g) garlic powder

This recipe is perfect for picky eaters. But for fun, play it cool and don't tell them what they're eating before they try a bite. Later you can congratulate them for eating loads of veggies.

Directions

1. Preheat the oven to 375 F (190 C), or preheat the grill.

2. Line a large baking sheet with parchment paper and spray with olive oil.

3. In a large bowl, combine cauliflower rice with ground beef and seasonings. Roll into 8 to 16 balls and place on a baking sheet.

4. Lay a sheet of parchment paper across the top of all the burgers and use a flat spatula to press down on each ball to form a flat burger patty.

5. Keeping the parchment paper on, bake for 20 to 23 minutes, depending on the size and level of doneness desired. Alternatively, cook them on a grill.

Note: If using a grill, I recommend using a flat top cooking surface or cooking the burgers in a cast-iron skillet.

Serve in a lettuce wrap or a high fiber bun with sprouts, pickles, avocado, ketchup, mustard, and tomato.

If making these for picky eaters, be sure to grate the cauliflower into very fine small pieces.

MAPLE CRUSTED AIR FRIED SALMON

Serves 3–4

1 pound (454g) salmon filets

1½ tsps. (7.5g) Dijon mustard

1 tbsp. (15ml) maple syrup, date syrup, or monk fruit syrup

1 tsp. (5ml) coconut aminos or low sodium soy sauce

1 tsp. (3g) garlic, minced

Salt and pepper to taste

Red chili flakes (optional)

This is a sweet and savory salmon that gets super sticky and crispy in the air fryer. Turn it into an easy dinner by doubling the marinade recipe and tossing it with chopped broccoli, fennel, or tri-colored peppers. Cook vegetables in the air fryer alongside the salmon.

Directions

1. Preheat oven or air fryer to 375 F (190 C).

2. Mix maple syrup, Dijon mustard, coconut aminos, and garlic in a small bowl.

3. Rub the maple mixture over salmon with a brush or spoon, or using clean, washed hands if you like.

4. Air fry for 12 to 15 minutes at 375 F (190 C), or place in a baking dish in the oven for 20 to 25 minutes.

Note: Use grainy stone-ground Dijon mustard for deeper flavor.

CRISPY HONEY MUSTARD CHICKEN NUGGETS

Serves 3–4

1 lb. (454g) boneless skinless chicken breast, cubed into one to two inch pieces

2 tsps. (30ml) olive oil

1½ tsps. (2.5g) garlic powder

1½ tsps. (3.3g) smoked paprika

½ tsp. (1.2g) onion powder

½ tsp. (1.2g) tomato powder (optional)

½ cup (60g) breadcrumbs, divided

2 tbsps. (42g) honey

2 tbsps. (30g) Dijon mustard

Scallions for garnish (optional)

Directions

1. Add chicken to a large mixing bowl with olive oil and toss well.

2. In a small mixing bowl, combine the garlic, paprika, and onion powder, and sprinkle mixture onto the chicken. Mix well until all the chicken is evenly coated with seasoning.

3. Add mustard and honey over the chicken with half the breadcrumbs (¼ cup/30g). Chicken should be coated with the wet honey mustard mixture. Sprinkle remaining breadcrumbs over the chicken for a slightly dryer outer coating.

4. Preheat the air fryer to 400 F (205 C) and spray with avocado, olive, or coconut oil spray. Place the chicken in the basket and spray the top of the chicken with additional oil spray.

5. Cook the chicken in an even layer for 10 to 13 minutes in an air fryer, or bake in the oven on a greased baking sheet for 20 to 25 minutes.

Note: To make these a little spicy, replace the honey in the recipe with 1 tbsp. (21g) honey mixed with 1 tbsp. (21g) hot honey.

CHICKEN MARSALA

Serves 4–6

8 pieces chicken, cut up with skin removed

½ cup (65g) whole wheat or gluten free flour

1 tsp. (1.6g) garlic powder

1 tsp. (2.2g) paprika

½ tsp. (2g) dried thyme

½ tsp. (2.8g) salt

½ tsp. (0.1g) black pepper

2 cups (473ml) chicken or vegetable broth

¼ cup (60ml) marsala wine or cooking wine of your choice

3 tbsps. (45ml) olive oil, divided

2 onions, sliced

3 stalks of celery, chopped

1 8-oz. box mushrooms (225g), sliced

3 cloves garlic, chopped

¼ cup (10g) dried porcini mushrooms for extra flavor (optional)

Fresh parsley for garnish

My childhood friend Caroline always had this chicken marsala in her fridge. It is so delicious that even as we've gotten older, I'd ask her to bring me the leftovers from her parents' house. It was one of the first recipes I made for my husband when we got married twelve years ago, and he still asks me to make it every fall and winter.

Directions

1. Preheat the oven to 400 F (205 C).

2. In a large mixing bowl, add flour, garlic powder, paprika, thyme, salt, and pepper.

3. Mix well, then coat raw chicken pieces well with the flour mixture.

4. In a large ceramic pot, add 2 tbsps. (30ml) olive oil and bring to medium heat.

5. Add the flour-coated chicken to the hot pot and brown the chicken for 2 to 3 minutes on each side, then place the chicken on a separate dish. (Add the chicken pieces in batches so you don't crowd the pot.)

6. Once all the chicken has been browned, add the remaining oil to the pot, then add the chopped garlic.

7. Cook until fragrant, about one minute, then add the onions, celery, and mushrooms.

8. Use a rubber spatula to scrape down the browned bits on the bottom of the pan while constantly stirring the vegetables.

9. Bring the heat down to low to medium and cook until the onions have wilted, about 4 to 5 minutes.

10. Add the broth and wine and stir.

11. Next, add the chicken back to the pot, and add dried porcini mushrooms if using.

12. Cover and place in the oven for one hour.

13. Enjoy!

SAUCES AND DIPS

FOR PERFECT PAIRINGS WITH
YOUR FAVORITE VEGGIES & PROTEINS

PICKLED ONIONS

Serves 8–10

½ cup (120ml) apple cider vinegar or white vinegar

½ cup (120ml) boiling water

2 tbsps. (34g) salt

1 tbsp. (13g) sugar

2 red onions, sliced thin

1–3 cloves garlic (optional)

Directions

1. Add vinegar, hot water, salt, and sugar to a Mason jar or bowl and stir.

2. Add in onions, submerging them under the liquid.

3. Cover tightly and refrigerate for at least 30 minutes (or up to five days).

4. Serve on salads, over eggs, in stir fries, on wraps, and in bowls.

5. Veggie variation: Replace the onions in this recipe with another veggie; consider sliced Persian cucumber spears, radishes, or peeled turnips sliced into sticks.

Pro Tip: For a fast and fantastic shortcut, reuse your favorite pickling liquid. Next time you finish a jar of pickles, add sliced onions, cucumbers, cauliflower, or other sturdy veggies of your choice straight to the jar. These make the easiest repurposed pickles.

HERB RANCH DIP

Serves 6–8

6 oz. (170g) plain yogurt (Greek or dairy free as you prefer)

Juice of 1 lemon, about 3 tbsp. (45ml)

¼-½ cup (15–30g) or generous handfuls of chopped fresh herbs like dill, parsley, or cilantro

2 garlic cloves, minced

Salt and pepper to taste

Directions

1. In a bowl, mix the ingredients together.

2. Enjoy with any sliced or roasted veggie!

MISO GINGER DIP

Serves 6–8

¼ cup (60ml) avocado or olive oil

¼ cup (60ml) rice vinegar

2 carrots, chopped

1 inch (3cm) fresh ginger root

3 tbsps. (50g) miso paste

1 tbsp. (21g) honey or stevia to taste

Directions

1. Blend all ingredients in a blender or food processor.

2. Enjoy as a dip or dressing for veggies or over a protein like tofu or salmon.

SWEET BALSAMIC "SPECIAL SAUCE"

Serves 4

¼ cup (60ml) balsamic vinegar

1 tbsp. (15g) Dijon mustard

1 tbsp. (20g) strawberry jam, honey, or coconut sugar

Salt and pepper

2 tbsps. (30ml) olive oil (optional)

Directions

1. In a bowl, mix the above ingredients.

2. Enjoy over a big salad, quinoa, or roasted veggies, or use it as a marinade for chicken, meat, or fish. The versatility makes it so special.

> **Tip:** The oil is optional because sometimes you don't need it. For example, if I'm using it over a salad with tuna mixed with mayo, I find it doesn't need the added richness.

MAPLE TAHINI DIP

Serves 4–6

¼ cup (60g) tahini

¼ cup (60ml) rice or apple cider vinegar

2–3 tbsps. (30–45ml) hot water

2–3 tbsps. (30–45ml) maple syrup

1 tbsp. (15g) Dijon mustard

1 pinch salt

Directions

1. In a bowl, mix the above ingredients.

2. Enjoy with boiled or roasted brussels sprouts and green beans, or accompanying any veggie of your choosing.

Love the Food that Loves You Back

MAPLE TAHINI SALAD DRESSING

Serves 8–10

⅓ cup (80g) tahini

⅓ cup (80ml) apple cider vinegar

⅓ cup (80ml) maple syrup or monk fruit syrup

½ cup (120ml) hot water (the warmth helps thins out the tahini sauce)

2 cloves garlic, chopped

Salt and pepper to taste

Directions

1. Combine all ingredients in a bowl and whisk.

2. This dressing is perfect over an array of salad greens.

Note: For the dressing, start with ⅓ cup water (80ml) and add more for liquidity as desired.

SPICY MAYO

Serves 1–2

2 tbsps. (30g) light or Japanese mayonnaise

1 tsp. (5ml) sriracha

½ tsp. (2.5ml) rice vinegar

½ tsp. (2.5ml) chili oil (optional)

Directions

1. Mix and enjoy with lots of dipper veggies, or make your own version of a poké style bowl with cauliflower or hearts of palm rice, avocado, cucumber, carrot, and sliced tofu or fish!

HIGH PROTEIN FRENCH ONION DIP

Serves 16

3 yellow onions, chopped

2 tsps. (10g) coconut oil

1 cup (280g) plain low-fat or nonfat Greek yogurt (or silken tofu)

2 tbsps. (30g) light mayonnaise

1½ tbsps. (5g) chives, chopped

1 tsp. (1.6g) garlic powder

½ tsp. (2.8g) salt

¼ tsp. (0.6g) black pepper

Chopped fresh parsley or pickled onion for garnish (Optional)

This is a perfect dip for a brunch or party. Everyone will be obsessed with it.

Directions

1. Heat a large pan over low to medium heat.

2. Add coconut oil and onions and cook, stirring every 1 to 3 minutes for 30 to 60 minutes.

3. Once the onions are deep brown and caramelized, add them to a bowl with the rest of the ingredients. Stir to combine, then garnish with additional chopped chives and serve with cucumbers and whole grain tortilla chips. This dip even shines as a topper for grilled chicken.

Note: The lower and slower the onions caramelize, the more flavorful they become, so be patient and don't take them off the stove until they are deep in color.

BANGIN' BABA GANOUSH

Serves 16

2 globe eggplant, pierced with a knife or fork

½ tsp. (0.8g) garlic powder

¼-½ tsp. (1.4–2.8g) salt

2 heaping tbsps. (35g) tahini

Juice of one lemon

3 tbsps. (12g) fresh parsley, chopped

1–3 tbsps. (15–45ml) water

½ tsp. (1.5g) cumin (optional but highly recommended)

¼ tsp. (0.5g) sumac (optional)

This baba ganoush is so amazing, I love making it for guests and sharing it with friends. It also lasts up to five days in your refrigerator so it's great to make in advance for a party. If you love Indian food, take it from me and add an extra ½–1 tsp. (2.5–5g) curry spice to it—it's amazing.

Directions

1. Preheat oven to 400 degrees F (205 C).

2. Place eggplants on a baking sheet lined with tin foil or parchment paper and cook for 45 minutes to an hour.

3. You should be able to pierce the eggplants easily with a fork, and the skin and flesh should be very tender and soft. Set aside to cool.

4. In a small bowl, whisk water and tahini until combined. In a large bowl or plate, scoop out the flesh of the eggplants while removing the seeds, then whisk or blend the flesh with the remaining ingredients.

5. Feel free to add more or less of each ingredient to taste.

BEST SWEET TAHINI DRESSING

Serves 1–2

Juice of ½ lemon

2 tbsps. (30g) tahini

1 tbsp. (22g) honey

1 tsp. (15g) Dijon mustard

Pinch salt and pepper

Directions

1. In a bowl, mix the above ingredients together.

2. Enjoy with any sliced or roasted veggie, protein, or fiber filled carbohydrate.

SAVVY
SWEETS

COTTAGE CHEESE STRAWBERRY ICE CREAM

Serves 2–4

2 cups (450g) low-fat cottage cheese

1 cup (150g) frozen strawberries

2 tbsps. (2g) puffed whole grain cereal

2 tbsps. (20g) crushed freeze-dried strawberries

2 tbsps. (42g) honey

About 8 drops of stevia to taste

1 tsp. (5ml) vanilla

This isn't exactly like strawberry cheesecake ice cream, but it sure comes close and hits the spot!! If you freeze it for longer than the recipe recommends, simply allow time for it to defrost on the counter for five or so minutes before scooping.

Directions

1. Blend cottage cheese with honey, vanilla, and stevia to taste. Pour half of the mixture out into a resealable container and freeze. Add frozen strawberries to the remaining cottage cheese, honey, and vanilla mixture and blend again. Pour this pink cottage cheese mixture into a separate resealable bowl or container. Freeze both for two to three hours.

2. When soft and frozen, serve a scoop of each and top with a sprinkle of puffed cereal and freeze-dried strawberries.

WATERMELON CAKE

Serves 4–6

1 small watermelon

1 cup (225g)
  cottage cheese

2–3 tbsps. (25–40g)
  coconut sugar or
  monk fruit sweetener,
  or 1–2 tsps. (5–10ml)
  liquid stevia

1 tsp. (5ml) vanilla extract

¼ cup (50g) toppings:
  your choice of crushed
  nuts, blueberries,
  sliced strawberries,
  sliced bananas, natural
  sprinkles, and dark
  chocolate chips

Among my nieces and nephews and their friends, I'm famous for this cake. Don't get me wrong, my family still loves traditional cake, but when it comes to making a special moment for a birthday party, there's nothing kids think is cooler than a cake made out of watermelon. If needed, you can definitely use regular frosting, just make sure you frost the "cake" immediately before serving because the wet watermelon doesn't adhere to any kind of frosting for very long.

Directions

1. Cut two to three inches off both ends of the watermelon, then place one flat side of the watermelon down on a cutting board.

2. Using a sharp knife, carefully trim the rind off the sides of the clean watermelon and place on a plate. Pat as dry as you can with paper towels.

3. In a blender add cottage cheese, vanilla, and stevia to create "whipped cream" frosting.

4. Frost watermelon and decorate with strawberries, blueberries, and toppings!

ALLERGY-FRIENDLY CHOCOLATE DISCS

Serves 4

½ cup (85g) dark chocolate chips

1 tbsp. (14g) coconut oil

⅓ cup (70g) pomegranate seeds, diced berries, or sliced bananas

¼ cup (35g) pumpkin seeds, sunflower seeds, or coconut flakes

1 tsp. (3g) flaky sea salt

I love making these for a crowd because they are beautiful and can be made dairy free (just look for vegan dark chocolate), gluten free, and nut free. Plus it's chocolate, so everyone's happy.

Directions

1. Line a cupcake pan with cupcake liners. In a microwave-safe bowl, mix chocolate chips and coconut oil, then microwave in 30-second intervals for one to two minutes. After each 30-second interval, use a metal fork to stir the chocolate and coconut oil mixture until completely melted and smooth.

2. Slowly pour 1 tablespoon of dark chocolate into each cupcake liner.

3. While the chocolate is still warm, top with ½–1 tsp. (1–2g) of fruit, a sprinkle of seeds, and a dusting of flaky sea salt in each cupcake liner.

4. Freeze for at least an hour before serving; store in an airtight container in the freezer for up to three months.

Love the Food that Loves You Back

CHOCOLATE PEANUT BUTTER MUG CAKE

Serves 1

2 tbsps. (30g) peanut butter powder

1½ tbsp. (19g) monk fruit sweetener or coconut sugar

2 tsps. (5g) cocoa powder

¼ tsp. (2g) baking soda

Pinch of salt

2 tbsps. (30ml) unsweetened almond milk or milk of your choice

1 tsp. (5ml) olive, coconut, or avocado oil

1 tsp. (5ml) vanilla extract

When you want peanut butter cake...make this on repeat.

Directions

1. Combine the peanut butter powder, sweetener, cocoa powder, baking soda, and salt in the bottom of a microwavable mug or bowl, stirring to remove any lumps.

2. Add in the milk, oil, and vanilla, and stir until smooth and uniform.

3. Microwave for 45 seconds. Let cool and serve with a sprinkle of powdered sugar (optional).

Note: This sweet and light treat is a lot of fun. If you have a sweet tooth, this is a satisfying way to crush your chocolate and cake cravings all at once. It also has three grams of fiber and can be used as an FFC serving with the 2B Mindset® program. You can even add berries and a cup of Greek yogurt to turn this into a complete breakfast.

NICE CREAM

Serves 3–4

3 bananas, sliced
  and frozen

¼ cup (60ml) almond milk

1 tsp. (5ml) vanilla, almond,
  or cake batter extracts

½ tsp. (1.5g) cinnamon

Directions

1. Blend all ingredients together and enjoy
    with cacao nibs, crushed nuts, or toppings of
    your choice.

Notes: To make it festively seasonal for autumn:
Substitute ¼ cup (60g) pumpkin purée in place of
almond milk and add ½ tsp. (1.5g) pumpkin pie spice

To make it tropical: Add ½ cup (45g) of chopped
mango, blueberries, or sliced strawberries.

To amp up the protein: Add a scoop of protein
powder or 1 cup (280g) Greek yogurt or silken tofu.

CHOCOLATE COCONUT DREAM PIE

Serves 6–8

2 cups (140g) shredded
  unsweetened
  coconut flakes

11 dates

3 cups (840g)
  Greek yogurt

¼ cup (30g) cocoa powder

1 tsp. (5ml) stevia or monk
  fruit extract

1 tsp. (5ml) vanilla extract

3 tbsps. (45g) dark
  chocolate chips

1 tbsp. (14g) coconut oil

1 tbsp. (5g) coconut flakes
  for garnish

Directions

1. Make the crust by blending the coconut flakes with the dates in a blender or food processor. Press the mixture into the bottom of a pie dish or into 8 mini Mason jars for individual servings.

2. Clean out the blender, then add the Greek yogurt, cocoa powder, vanilla, and stevia to it. Mix well and pour out mixture on top of the pie crust.

3. In a microwave-safe bowl, add the chocolate chips and coconut oil. Microwave for a minute, stopping halfway to stir.

4. Microwave for an additional 30 seconds, stirring often until the oil and chocolate are well combined.

5. Drizzle the chocolate mixture over the yogurt.

6. To make a marble top design, use your knife to swirl figure eights throughout the yogurt.

7. Sprinkle with coconut flakes for garnish. Refrigerate for 2 hours before serving. Serve cold.

Note: You can reduce the amount of chocolate drizzle topping and turn this into a healthy and complete high protein breakfast. If eating it as a breakfast, the serving size would be about one-fourth of the pie.

LITTLE RUTHIE'S MINI BLUEBERRY MUFFINS

Serves 12

6 tbsps. (90ml) melted coconut oil or olive oil, plus more for greasing pans

1½ cups (420g) Greek yogurt or silken tofu

2 tsps. (8g) lemon zest (grated from the skin of 1 medium lemon)

1 large egg

⅔ cup (134g) coconut sugar or sugar in the raw

1½ tsps. (7g) baking powder

¼ tsp. (1.5g) baking soda

¼ tsp. (1.4g) salt

1½ cups (195g) whole wheat flour or one-to-one gluten free flour

2 cups (380g) fresh or frozen blueberries, strawberries, or bananas, finely chopped

These taste so much like those little white bags of blueberry muffins we all love so much, but you and your picky eater friends will have no clue that there's an added boost of protein baked into the batter.

Directions

1. Preheat oven to 425 F (220 C). Grease a mini cupcake pan.

2. In a large bowl, mix oil, Greek yogurt, sugar, lemon zest, egg, baking powder, baking soda, and salt. Mix well until combined. In a separate bowl, toss together blueberries and flour until each berry is covered. Slowly pour floured blueberries into the yogurt mixture and stir until combined. Using a mini scooper or spoon, add about two tablespoons of batter into each mini muffin cup. Bake for 23 to 25 minutes.

3. Or use as pancake batter.

> **Note:** I use frozen wild blueberries and make this year-round. This batter can also work as a pancake batter if you prefer to make it on a stove top.

SOUR CANDY GRAPE STICKS

Serves 3–6

3 cups (450g) whole fresh green grapes

1 tbsp. (2g) fresh mint, chopped

1 tbsp. (13g) sugar

1–3 tsps. (15–45ml) lime juice (more if you want it extra sour)

1 large (1-gallon/378ml) zip-sealable plastic bag

About six 4-inch skewers (optional)

My friend Reva shared this recipe with me, and it quickly made my mouth water at the thought of enjoying this on a hot summer day. I hope you'll feel the same way. It's great to store in the freezer for whenever you are looking for something sweet.

Directions

1. To a large resealable bag, add grapes, mint, sugar, and lime juice. Shake very well.

2. Pierce the mixed grapes on skewers and secure in a food storage container. Freeze for at least 2 hours before serving.

MIMI'S EASY YUMMY PIE

Serves 8

1½ cups (195g) whole wheat or gluten free flour

1 tsp. (5g) baking powder

¾ cup (150g) coconut sugar, or equivalent quantity of natural low-calorie sweetener

1 egg

½ cup (120g) melted coconut oil

½ tsp. (3g) vanilla

1 16-oz. (454g) bag of frozen wild blueberries *or* one-lb. (454g) container of fresh blueberries *or* 4–5 sliced apples (or combine both blueberries and apples)

Directions

1. Preheat oven to 350 F (175 C). Add all of the ingredients except the fruit to a bowl and mix well to form the dough. Spray a pie dish with oil. Spread ¾ of the dough on the bottom of the dish. Use your hands to press the dough down and make an even crust. Add blueberries or apples on top of the crust.

2. Using your fingers, crumble the remaining ¼ dough and scatter along the top of the fruit. Bake for 40 min.

Note: If using sweet red apples, add the juice of half a lemon to bring some tartness to the dish and help prevent browning.

ACKNOWLEDGEMENTS

First and foremost, I would like to acknowledge my amazing social media followers, who were relentless about telling me how much I needed to publish a cookbook these past few years. Without your comments, kindness, support, and enthusiasm, this would not have been possible.

I would like to thank my husband, Noah, the grill master, and our three amazing children, Olivia, Julian, and Gideon, who have been unapologetically forthright with their honest critiques and feedback. (Chicken Chomp truly is their favorite recipe in the book, so be sure to check it out on page 123.) You are all the loves of my life.

I want to express my appreciation to:

My mom, Z"l, who always showed me that there's no shame in kitchen shortcuts like frozen vegetables and bottled sauces; my dad, for inspiring me to pursue my passions, and for becoming a health warrior in his later years, celebrating his vitality, and going to Pilates every day.

To my mother-in-law, Perla, a true Balabusta (Yiddish for homemaker), and my father-in-law, Herman: Your home is always filled with food that is not only delicious and abundant, but is served at the perfect temperature, in the best serving dishes, and paired with the perfect wine, beer, or cocktail accompaniment.

To my four incredible siblings, my seven sisters and brothers-in-law, and fourteen nieces and nephews: Our family means the world to me, and I hope to enjoy hundreds more wonderful meals together in our future.

To my friends for constantly sharing your recipes, making me laugh, and being a shoulder to cry on: I consider so many of you my sisters from another mister and am so grateful for our friendships.

This book would not be possible without my incredible book agent, Alison, my publisher, my team at Mango, and my food photographer, Corinne. Corinne reached out to us precisely at the time we were looking for a food photographer. She was struggling with her weight and emotional eating habits at the same time she was launching her food styling career.

Here is a note Corinne wanted to share with you of her personal experience working on this book.

The last few years I've been up and down with my weight, dealing with typical life stressors as we all do. One thing that I always end up going to back to is stress eating or emotional eating. I'm the worst with that!

When I first took on this project, I was so excited for the opportunity to work with Ilana and try firsthand the recipes that help thousands of people lose weight and keep it off. I've followed Ilana for years but never really tried any recipes until working on the cookbook!

Not only are the recipes jam packed with protein, fiber, and nutrients, but they're all so delicious! There are recipes for literally everyone in this book. Even if you're a picky eater, they're all easy to make.

I gained a really deep understanding of my relationship with food throughout this project, and I definitely owe it to Ilana's' methods. Following the water first and veggies most but also keeping the protein and fiber intake up too has helped keep me full and keep the cravings away. Not to mention that there are really delicious recipes for when I have a sweet tooth!!

In the past several weeks, following these recipes has given me a better relationship with food and my body and a better understanding of *how much* I'm eating. I've lost ten pounds while maintaining my current muscle mass, and more importantly, I'm feeling better than ever!

ABOUT THE AUTHOR

Dietitian, nutritionist, bestselling author, and mother of three Ilana Muhlstein, MS, RD, stands as a highly sought-after global health and wellness expert. Her success has been propelled by her personal, relatable weight loss journey and sharp intellect.

At just thirteen years of age, Ilana weighed over two hundred pounds, grappling with challenges such as emotional eating and the constant cycle of ineffective diets. Seizing the earliest opportunity to become a dietitian, Ilana applied all she learned to lose a hundred pounds and sustain her weight loss. Now, she is on a mission to demonstrate that leading a healthy lifestyle is easier and more attainable than many believe. Ilana derives joy from empowering individuals to break free from past insecurities and to step into the thrilling next chapters of their lives.

Since embarking on this mission, Ilana has held a lecturer position at the Bruin Health Improvement Program at UCLA since 2013. She contributes regularly to prestigious publications such as *The Journal of Obesity* and has had features in the *LA Times, The Washington Post, Reader's Digest, SHAPE, Health,* and *Women's Health.* Through her thriving private practice in Beverly Hills and a robust online presence boasting over three million followers, Ilana inspires her audience to reach their optimal health potential.

Ilana has spearheaded the bestselling weight loss program, "2B Mindset," and authored the hit book *You Can Drop It,* **which has sold over 50,000 copies**. Her relentless passion for helping others foster the best versions of themselves spurred the creation of more innovative tools, including Ilana Housewares (a houseware line designed for mindful consumption) and Ilana Meals (a meal delivery service). Both aimed at facilitating unnoticeable yet effective weight loss.

Ilana's educational background is rooted in a Bachelor of Science degree in nutrition and dietetics from the University of Maryland and a clinical dietetic internship at the City of Hope Medical Center, recognized as one of the top fifteen cancer hospitals in the US by US News and World Report. She further honed her expertise with a Master of Science degree in applied nutrition from Northeastern University.

Ilana currently resides in Los Angeles with her husband, Noah, and their three children: Oliva, Julian, and Gideon.

For more information about Ilana, visit www.ilanamuhlstein.com.

Love the Food that Loves You Back

FOR THE LATEST WEIGHT LOSS TIPS, MOTIVATIONAL NUTRITION NEWS, AND TRENDS IN HEALTH AND WELLNESS...

- Sign up for free weekly emails at www.ilanamuhlstein.com
- Follow Ilana on Instagram—www.instagram.com/ilanamuhlsteinrd
- Follow Ilana on Facebook—www.facebook.com/ilanamuhlstein
- Follow Ilana on TikTok—www.tiktok.com/nutritionbabe
- Follow along on YouTube—www.youtube.com/@IlanaMuhlsteinRD

TO LEARN MORE ABOUT ILANA'S PRODUCTS THAT CAN AID YOU IN YOUR WEIGHT-LOSS JOURNEY...

- Check out Ilana Housewares—www.ilanahousewares.com

NEED A BREAK FROM COOKING? THAT'S OKAY! LET ILANA TAKE CARE OF IT FOR YOU. TO LEARN MORE ABOUT ILANA MEALS DELIVERED STRAIGHT TO YOUR DOOR...

- Head to www.ilanameals.com

Scan Me for Discounts

INDEX

A

Almonds 93-94, 153
Apple 84, 90, 97, 173, 213
Avocado 73, 90, 106, 115, 127, 135, 140, 177, 179, 191

B

Bacon 60, 83
Banana 19, 163, 199-200, 204, 209
Basil 37, 41-43, 76, 97, 109, 112, 138
BBQ sauce 115, 123, 170
Beans, black 80, 135
Beef 109-110, 128, 170, 179
Beet 73, 87, 98
Bell pepper 22-23, 49, 69, 73-74, 76, 79, 94, 116, 138, 167, 173
Blueberries 73, 93, 153-154, 157, 199, 204, 209, 213
Bread 25, 169
  Cloud bread, see *Cloud Bread and variations*
  English muffin 21-22
  Sourdough 22, 100
Breadcrumbs 45, 55, 121, 123, 176-177, 183
Breakfast 17-29, 143, 169, 203, 206
Broccoli 47, 73, 128, 138, 180
Broth 109, 123, 184-185
Brussels sprouts 60, 87, 94, 190

C

Cabbage 73, 89, 93-94, 105, 115, 131, 170, 176
Carrot 23, 64, 73, 79-80, 87, 93-94, 106, 118, 123, 128, 170, 173, 189, 191
Cauliflower 70-71, 109-110, 124-125, 188, 191
  Cauliflower rice 59, 106, 118, 179
Celery 73, 123, 167, 173, 184
Cheese 135, 167
  Cheddar 124
  Cottage cheese 22, 26, 29, 73, 197, 199
  Cream cheese 59, 147
  Feta 42, 73-74, 80, 88
  Goat 84, 97
  Mozzarella 23, 51-52, 105, 112, 124, 138, 176
  Parmesan 37, 45, 55, 59, 98, 105, 112, 121
  Pecorino Romano 41
  Ricotta 105
Chia seeds 29, 144
Chickpeas 88, 100

Chicken 43, 63, 73, 80, 83, 100, 109, 115-116, 121, 123, 131, 176, 183-185, 190, 193
Chives 22, 41, 47, 71, 147, 169, 193
Chocolate 19, 26, 163-164, 199-200, 203, 206
  Cocoa powder 19, 203, 206
  Cacao nibs 163, 204
Cilantro 52, 67, 80, 115, 124-125, 189
Cloud Bread and variations 133-147
Coconut flakes 200, 206
Coconut milk 106, 109-110
Corn 80, 115
Cornstarch 37, 52, 128, 134-147
Crab 106, 127
Cucumber 74, 76, 79, 80, 84, 88-89, 94, 97, 100, 106, 127, 188, 191, 193

D

Date 94, 206
Desserts 196-213
Dijon mustard 74, 83, 97, 100, 167, 177, 180, 183, 190, 195
Dill 167, 174, 176-177, 189
Dinners, see *Lunches and Dinners*

E

Egg 19, 22-23, 25, 45, 59, 83, 105-106, 109, 118, 128, 167, 169, 176-177, 188, 209, 213
  Egg white 20, 22, 25-26, 134-147
Eggplant 38, 45, 63, 121, 194
English muffin, see *Bread*
"Everything" bagel seasoning 56, 63, 70, 147

F

Fries 45, 56
FroWhoas 159-164

G

Ginger root 79, 189
Green beans 69, 190
Green onion 33, 38, 47, 93-94, 106-107, 118, 128, 167, 169, 177, 183

H

Hearts of palm 33, 43, 55, 100, 118, 191
Hemp seeds 87, 89, 94
Honey 19, 29, 60, 74, 76, 79-80, 84, 94, 97, 144, 183, 189-190, 195, 197

K

Kale 84, 87, 89-90, 131, 138
Kelp noodles 42-43
Kiwi 29

Love the Food that Loves You Back

L

Lemon 110, 121, 147, 153, 174, 177, 209
  Lemon juice 41, 67, 83, 87-90, 93, 98, 100, 106, 115-116, 127, 140, 153, 167, 176-177, 189, 194-195, 213
Lettuce 21, 73-76, 83, 100, 115-116, 127, 179
Lime 124-125, 128
  Lime juice 76, 80, 210
Lunches and Dinners 102-131

M

Marinara sauce 45, 51, 55, 105, 112, 121, 138
Mayonnaise 21, 83, 98, 100, 106, 115, 127, 167, 169, 190-193
Mint 67, 88, 97, 210
Miso 79, 106-107, 127, 131, 189
Mushroom 22, 49, 51, 98, 109-110, 116, 128, 138, 184-185

N

Nutritional yeast 41, 100, 118-119

O

Oats 20
Olives 52, 74, 138
Orange, mandarin 67, 79, 93
Oregano 42, 59, 74, 100, 109, 112, 118, 121

P

Papaya 29
Parsley 67, 71, 88, 109-110, 115-116, 121, 167, 184, 189, 193-194
Pasta swaps 31-43
Peanuts 33, 94, 128, 150, 164
Peanut butter 33, 94
  Peanut butter powder 128, 144, 150, 164, 203
Pear 90, 97, 173
Pomegranate seeds 64, 84, 94, 200
Potato 23
Protein powder 149, 160-164, 204
Pumpkin seeds 67, 89, 200

R

Ranch 47, 56, 189
Raspberries 144, 154
Rutabaga 56, 173

S

Salads, Sexy 37, 73-100
Salmon 106, 127, 147, 174, 177, 180, 189
Salsa 52, 135
Sauces and Dips 187-195
Scallion, see green onion

Sesame seeds 38, 106, 118
Shirataki noodles 41, 128
Soy sauce 33, 38, 79, 84, 87, 94, 106, 118, 127-128, 173, 180
Spaghetti squash 34-35, 37, 43
Spinach 23, 79, 97
Stevia 19, 26, 79, 94, 137, 143, 150, 153-154, 157, 160, 163, 189, 197, 199, 206
Strawberries 29, 73, 157, 190, 197, 199, 204, 209
Stock, see Broth
Sunflower seeds 76, 89, 94, 200
Sweet potato 29

T

Tahini 64, 87, 116, 190-191, 194-195
Tajin seasoning 52, 67, 124
Tempeh 21, 121
Teriyaki sauce 64, 170
Thyme 109-110, 173, 184
Tofu 43, 73-74, 79, 83, 106-107, 112, 116, 118-119, 121, 127, 149, 176, 189, 191, 193, 204, 209
Tomato 21-22, 73-74, 80, 90, 115, 124, 140, 169, 179
  Cherry tomatoes 41-42, 74, 83, 88-89, 94, 100, 140
  Tomato sauce, see Marinara sauce
Tuna 80, 116, 127, 167, 176-177, 190
Turnip 56, 173, 188
Turkey 60, 83, 109, 124, 173

W

Walnut 41, 74, 84, 97
Wonder Whips 149-157

Y

Yogurt 29, 47, 137, 149, 189
  Greek yogurt 19, 25, 29, 83, 106, 124-125, 137, 150, 153-154, 157, 167, 176-177, 189, 193, 203-204, 206, 209

Z

Zucchini 112, 161, 163-164

Mango Publishing, established in 2014, publishes an eclectic list of books by diverse authors—both new and established voices—on topics ranging from business, personal growth, women's empowerment, LGBTQ studies, health, and spirituality to history, popular culture, time management, decluttering, lifestyle, mental wellness, aging, and sustainable living. We were named 2019 *and* 2020's #1 fastest growing independent publisher by *Publishers Weekly*. Our success is driven by our main goal, which is to publish high-quality books that will entertain readers as well as make a positive difference in their lives.

Our readers are our most important resource; we value your input, suggestions, and ideas. We'd love to hear from you—after all, we are publishing books for you!

Please stay in touch with us and follow us at:

Facebook: Mango Publishing
Twitter: @MangoPublishing
Instagram: @MangoPublishing
LinkedIn: Mango Publishing
Pinterest: Mango Publishing
Newsletter: mangopublishinggroup.com/newsletter

Join us on Mango's journey to reinvent publishing, one book at a time.